C000272445

When Dad
BECAME JOAN

Life with
My Transgender father

Cath Lloyd
Living with normal

Copyright © 2017 by Cath Lloyd. All rights reserved. This book or any portion thereof may not be reproduced or used in any manner whatsoever without the express written permission of the publisher except for the use of brief quotations in a book review.

Printed in the United Kingdom

Cover illustration by Katharine Skorka
katharineskorka@gmail.com

First Printing, 2017

ISBN 978-0-9957390-8-6 (Paperback)
ISBN 978-0-9957390-9-3 (Ebook)

Librotas Books
Portsmouth, Hampshire
PO2 9NT

www.LibrotasBooks.com

Contents

Part ONE:
The day I learned a new normal

Part Two:
7 steps to living your new normal

Acknowledgements

This year is the 30th anniversary of my dad coming out as a transsexual. I would like to acknowledge and celebrate how far we have come as a family.

First and foremost, I would like to thank my parents for being who they are. For being strong and helping us to stay together as a family through what could have been a disastrous family life. If they hadn't met or if Dad had followed his dream of being Joan earlier in their life I would never have been born. I would also like to thank them for agreeing to me writing this book and supporting me through the process.

Without my mentor Karen Williams, this book would never have started. Her continual patience and gentle yet challenging questioning enabled me to finally develop the trust I needed to unpack the past and say what I was really thinking. Karen helped me start forming the words to a story that I had been denying to myself for many years. To my editor Esther Harris for her expert advice and sharing her wealth of experience.

Huge acknowledgements also to my husband Nick for allowing me to tap away and soothe my angst and frustrations, with his trademark sense of humour keeping everything in place as usual. His unwavering emotional and practical support in allowing me to continuously let go and download whilst giving me countdowns to meal times with the perfect quantity of hugs and kisses was incredible. Thanks to my daughter Jess for all her IT skills, her questioning of my ideas and her ability and willingness to indulge me in challenging my conflicting arguments to help me see things more clearly. For Pete, my son, for just being who he is.

I would also like to thank the family, friends and professionals who have taken part in this book. For talking with me, being open and honest with me and giving me the support that I needed. I really appreciate the time spent and you will never know how valuable your support has been to me.

I feel it's also important to extend my gratitude to the family who felt they didn't want to share their deepest thoughts with me. I respect your feelings and appreciate your openness and honesty. This has been a challenging and frightening journey for some. Therefore, names and details have been changed to help them feel more secure in the knowledge that they can continue their life as they are, feeling happy.

Lastly, I would like to thank all those who have supported my family for the past 30 years, who stood by them in their private life and at work, accepted the changes that had to be made and respected the privacy that was needed. The love, kindness and respect you have shown over the years have earned my eternal gratefulness.

Thank you.

All my love Cath xxx

PART ONE

The day I learned
a new normal

> **"** There are good days
> And there are bad days,
> And this is one of them. **"**

Musician and TV impresario Lawrence Welk

PART ONE: The day I learned a new normal

Introduction

I approach the counter at the doctor's surgery. The receptionist smiles up at me.

"Hi, my name is Cath Lloyd and two of my relatives are patients here – Annie Homer and Joan Mason."

"OK, so Annie is your mother… and Joan is your sister." Not a question… a statement. Tap, tap, tap go her fingers on the keyboard.

I take a deep breath. This isn't going to go away. "No. Annie is my mother and Joan is my…"

She looks at me enquiringly. *Get a grip Cath*, I tell myself. *You have been avoiding this for thirty years.* I'm scared by what I think, and I'm scared by what other people might think too. In fact, I'm just scared of everything. Mind you, that is hardly surprising when what I trusted as 'normal' for so many years turned out to be wrong: a lie, a mix-up.

Life has certainly taught me one thing – none of us really knows what is going on deep inside. Inside other people's heads, bodies, families or homes. We are all living with our own version of normal. We adapt, we accept, we muddle along as best we can. What may seem normal to one will vary for somebody else. For a split second I think back and remember my dad as a lovely person; everyone in our family just wanted him to be happy.

I take a deep breath before I continue: "Joan was my dad."

"Oh. Okay, how can I help you?"

***

It has taken me a long time to decide to write this book. I felt that I lost the dad I had grown up with when he told me he had gender dysphoria and was undergoing gender reassignment to become a woman with immediate effect. The bottom fell out of my world that day and I was never given a chance to properly grieve for the loss of my dad. Instead I was told to "please keep this to yourself". I don't blame him anymore. I now understand that he lived through this at a different time; he was a teacher, a pillar of the community in a conservative suburb in the 1970s, a kind and hardworking man who only wanted to raise his family and do everything 'by the book'. So his internal conflict devastated him. I know he considered suicide on several occasions. Gender dysphoria back then was not what it is now. It wasn't common knowledge; people hadn't heard of it. There wasn't the language available to describe the experience, and there was little knowledge or understanding. There was only shame and a desire to hide feelings, keeping them buried deep inside. Until the 1970s, psychotherapy was the primary treatment for gender dysphoria and sought to help the person adjust to the gender they were born with. It was a seemingly impossible situation for all concerned. But not impossible; for all the trauma and heartache, my parents are still together and devoted to each other.

I still miss the dad I grew up with and have wanted him back so many times over the years, but occasionally I pause and think: OK, so what's the alternative? What if my dad hadn't had the courage to face his crisis and go through with becoming a woman? My life could have taken a very different turn, a more challenging turn. He could have committed suicide, become ill, or run off and left his family. I would be a different person now, telling a very different story. And what of my mum? She might have ended her relationship and left her two girls with a broken man. But she didn't – she married Martin, my dad, and decided to stay with him when he became Joan.

This is a multi-layered story of honesty, strength, forgiveness, courage, regret, horror, discomfort, and love. It is my story of finally being heard, and it is my dad's story of how he had no choice but to change.

"

This is my Vietnam
I'm at war
Life keeps on dropping bombs
And I keep score.

"

My Vietnam,
written by Alecia Moore and Linda Perry

The day I found out

10 July 1987. I was twenty-three. I had completed my degree that year and had returned home to get on with the next stage of my life, whatever that might be. I only had a vague plan; I wanted to continue being creative and express myself through hand built pots, sell them to craft galleries and become a famous potter like Lucie Rie, Mary Rogers, Peter Lane and Elizabeth Fritsch. Being away at college had been great; I had my own space, I saw my boyfriend regularly, and I made pots to my heart's content. When I was making pots I felt calm and at one with myself. I was in contact with something fluid, something I had learned how to manipulate and express myself through. Being in my creative world allowed me to escape, and it was an antidote to my life at home. When I was growing up I sensed the unspoken sadness and tension in my father even when I couldn't understand it or know about it. And there is no doubt that my creative life and pottery gave me a chance to soothe away some of that, and escape.

My parents were occasional visitors to my university studios. As teachers they were always keen to 'talk shop' with John, our head of department. John wasn't offered much of an opportunity to chat with parents so he loved the chance to show off his department. On the odd occasion my mum would visit alone. I never really questioned it at the time with my dad's busy work schedule. I loved seeing Mum and Dad and, of course, they took me for a great meal, which is guaranteed to be the quickest way to any student's heart.

Most of the time I would stay in touch with my parents, but there were a couple of occasions when I made a last-minute decision to come home. On one such day, I turned up on the doorstep, expecting to be welcomed with open arms, but I didn't get the welcome I had longed for. My mum answered the door with an angry and bewildered expression and a whole host of questions, like "Why didn't you tell us you were coming?" and "How long are you staying for?" And the memorable statement: "Cath, you can't just turn up. You must tell us when you are coming."

"Why?" I said. "This is my home, isn't it? I should be able to come home when I like."

"We would just like to know when you are coming, that's all."

I felt like doing an about-turn, heading straight out the door and never coming back. Eventually my dad appeared with a welcoming smile, trying to hide an anxious look on his face as if he was about to deliver some bad news but couldn't get the words out.

I was utterly confused and hurt by their reactions but tried to shrug it off and focus on the studio I was setting up in the garage at home. I had it all planned out. When I finished my course I would be tucked up in my workshop away from the unrest in the house, happily making pots in the garage, and I would spend most of my free time at my boyfriend's parents' house where, in contrast, I was always warmly welcomed. It was easier there: more relaxed, less underlying tension.

One particular July day after graduation, I was summoned by my dad to his office at home. My immediate thought was, *What have I done now?* A summoning to Dad's office was rare and serious – the last time I was eighteen years old and my parents had finally realised that I had been having sex with my boyfriend and wanted to share their unhappiness with me.

My dad's office was nothing fancy. None of the furniture matched; there was a practical beige carpet, polystyrene ceiling tiles and sunny yellow curtains surrounding a large window that overlooked the garden. That day I sat opposite my dad with my hands in my lap, looking out onto the lawn, while my mind was racing: was one of them poorly and going to die? Were my parents going to split up? There was certainly been a lot of tension in the house lately. But, if that was the case, why was Mum not in on the conversation? She was in the house but busying herself with things that mums usually busy themselves with.

Dad looked down at his clasped hands resting on his desk, as if trying to find the words he needed. It felt like an age before he started his story. My dad is a reflective person, so his sentences tend to be carefully planned, carefully worded. I later realised that he had had a lifetime to think about how he would approach this life-changing conversation with me. Eventually he turned his anxious gaze away from his hands and looked at me, slowly and precisely starting the conversation.

"Now you are living back at home, I thought I needed to explain something to you," he began slowly, his gaze roving around the office.

"What's happened Dad?" I asked, trying to read him.

There was a long pause, and then he began.

"Since about the age of five years old I have always felt as if I was somebody different. For all these years I have always tried to control and contain these feelings but it has now got to the stage that I can't do this any longer. I am desperate and can't go on any longer as I am." He paused to glance at me.

I could sense the weight of his words, and I began to feel dread. I waited for more, thoughts running through my mind like wildfire, as I began to get a bit panicky. *Oh my god he is going to leave Mum!* was my main thought.

Dad seemed to be steeling himself, so I did too. "I have decided to have a sex change," he announced slowly. "To undertake gender reassignment treatment."

Now he met my eye and gave me a tired and searching smile. I just looked at him. My mind was blank. I wasn't expecting that.

1 + 1 = ... What was the question again?

I found myself staring at the books and files on his shelves, looking for clues. Well, what do you say to something like that?

So I began to laugh.

This laughter soon dispersed as I saw the hurt and bewildered expression of my dad.

Even though I was laughing I could feel the tension rising up through me while at the same time past events were slotting uncomfortably into place. I began to understand why my parents needed me to call before I came home and not just turn up unexpectedly. Why I couldn't just bring a friend home with me as a last-minute decision like I had gone to my friends' houses.

As Dad sat opposite me and let the tsunami trickle through every cell of my consciousness, I gazed into the garden and wondered how life could change so completely in seconds. Did Mum know? Yes. Did my sister know? What about the rest of the family? And then my head gradually tuned back to what Dad was telling me in his usual calm, precise way.

"Your mum has known about this for the past ten years and I told your sister the other day while she was over," he said, as if he could see into my mind. "I will give your sister away at her wedding as I am but then after that I will begin to live my life as a woman. For a long while in the house I have been dressing in women's clothes. Part of me was hoping you would walk in on me and then I wouldn't have to say all of this." He gave a nervous laugh, which quickly died out as he took in my agonised expression. "I have to live my new life as a woman for at least a year before I can undergo any operations," he continued, perhaps realising that at this point I could only listen. "More recently I have been having a lot of destructive thoughts about ending my life and these feelings are getting stronger. The time is right for me to do this now. Your mother and I are going to stay together but I will have to resign from work and, at some point, try and look for another position. Your mother will stay working where she is. I will have to leave because otherwise it will be too difficult for her and the rest of the staff."

So my mum and dad had it all worked out, I reflected. They had been talking about this and planning it for YEARS.

Dad leaned forward in an attempt to close the physical and emotional crater I could feel widening between us. I guess the pressure to do what he had just done must have been immense. And then he asked me the million-dollar question: "Do you have any questions?"

As my head started spinning, I knew I had masses of them but my head was so mixed up I couldn't even begin to think what they were, so I weakly answered, "No."

But what my head was really saying was, if I don't agree with it, what will happen? Will it all stop and go away or will something worse happen? I don't want this to happen – but I don't want my dad to be so unhappy that he tries to end his life anyway. In fact, there was one other really big question in my mind, the one that probably mattered more than most. It was:

If you become somebody else, who will you be to me?

As two internally reflective thinkers, we sat like strangers with nothing more to say to each other. Dad waited for more. I looked at his hands, still clasped. The clock on the wall ticked. The trees in the garden waved in the breeze. In a matter of minutes the life I had taken for granted had changed beyond recognition.

I got up to go without a word and I was silently ushered out of the office. As I passed Mum in the kitchen, there was nothing we could find to say to each other. We were all roaming around in our own thoughts. When I left the house that day to go to see Nick, my parents felt like strangers to me.

> My dad + my mum + my sister + me = does it equal 4 any longer?

The last words that we exchanged at the front door I have never forgotten. "Cath, at the moment this is just between close family members, so, besides Nick, please keep this to yourself." There were no hugs or kisses. No suggestion of when I would be home next. As I tried desperately hard to avoid eye contact my mum looked close to tears. My dad's face held a sense of foreboding: like, what now?

The burden of keeping the family secret had begun.

> " You watching me
> Hanging by a string this time
> Don't, easily
> The climax of the perfect lie
> You watching me
> Hanging by a string this time
> Don't, easily
> My smile's worth a hundred lies. "

Sweet About Me written by Gabriella Cilmi, Nick Coler, Miranda Cooper, Brian Higgins, Timothy Larcombe and Tim Powell

The man I lost

My dad was born Martin Homer, on the outskirts of Cheshire in 1935. We lived in a comfortable home with a large garden in the West Midlands, near to where Annie and Martin met at university many years before. The garden gave me and my sister a great space to play and also a place to nurture our own home-grown vegetables. We were allowed our own little plots next to each other.

As a child I believed that my dad could do anything. Whenever something was broken I'd always announce, "It's ok. Daddy will fix it." My father was an incredibly practical man so I was usually right. Back then, I was a total daddy's girl. My earliest memories are of him sitting in his chair and me climbing onto his lap. If he was reading the newspaper, he'd open up his arms and I'd crawl under the paper and snuggle into him. If he was watching TV it didn't matter to me what he was watching as long as I was sitting on his lap. It made me feel safe and loved. In the evening my mum was often busy with tidying up the kitchen and preparing for the next day so I'd turn to my dad for affection. He always wore a suit with a narrow tie, and no aftershave. He just smelt clean, of my dad.

Dad grew up with three brothers who were all extremely sporty. On sports days at their school, the other parents knew where all the prizes would be going. That side of my father stayed with him and he always embraced outdoor pursuits. He loved walking, running, mountaineering and sailing, although looking back maybe he was trying to prove his masculinity. He was an average-sized man but very conscious of his appearance and he was almost fanatical about staying in shape, and very cleanly shaven until he decided to grow a beard. I remember when he grew his beard on a camping holiday; Mum walked on the other side of the road she was so embarrassed by it! If a new food craze emerged, he'd jump on the latest bandwagon. For a while everything in our house had to have bran in it. I think we even had bran and jam sandwiches! That obsessive side of Dad's personality was obviously what kept him going through the years. It gave him the ability to fastidiously cover up who he really was.

Dad was stronger than he looked, but the thing most people first noticed about him was his kind face with his green eyes, like mine, his full lips, like mine, strong teeth, like mine, fair skin that burned easily, like mine. People at the school where he taught would always comment on how caring and compassionate Dad was and that made me feel really proud. He could have a laugh and a joke with the kids' parents and he was incredibly popular with the staff. Like his own father, Dad was hardworking and empathic and he would happily go out of his way to help others. If one of his pupils was struggling to make sense of their schoolwork, Dad would give them extra lessons at lunchtimes to help them through their exams. Passion and dedication to the job came naturally to him. My parents worked in the same school but Dad was a governor too and would often be in meetings until 9pm.

My sister and I were desperate to spend more time with him so during the school holidays, or at weekends, he'd take us into school where he'd let us use the Gestetner to print the next week's worksheets, sharpen the pencils ready for a lesson drawing graphs and maps, tidy the classrooms and help him update the notice-boards. At night we'd stay up late so we could have dinner with him, which got us into trouble at school the next day for being tired. I didn't care if I was constantly yawning in class, as long as I could see my dad before I went to bed.

My favourite times were the holidays we shared together. Most of them were spent outdoors and we did a lot of camping in the Lake District, Wales or Scotland. Often we'd be stuck in a field in the middle of nowhere, but whatever happened, Dad would insist on making the best of it. There were times when Mum and Dad would carry us sleeping to the car, then stay awake all night desperately trying to hold down the tent in a howling gale. Dad was extremely capable, resourceful and flexible which meant he would never give up. No matter what happened, we stayed on holiday until the bitter end. I can only remember a few occasions when we abandoned our camping trips, and that was after we'd endured five days of solid rain in a soggy, muddy field and Mum had insisted on going home.

A lot of the fun of those holidays was playing with all the other kids on the campsites. We'd all work as a gang pushing the cars out of the mud when the weather was poor. Other kids from school would go abroad to nice hotels but instead we were in the middle of a field pushing a car to the exit! But we loved it. I hated all the walking though and would moan so Dad would try to take my mind off it by making me recite my times tables. Often other members of my family would join us on our camping trips. I remember camping in the middle of a field full of sheep in Pembrokeshire. My uncle and aunt arrived, and next my grandma and grandpa pulled up. One of the first things my granddad did was grab some shears from the back of his car to trim the grass around the tent.

When we got into sailing we'd go camping with a dinghy, just to make life even more challenging. Dad would patiently show us how to do everything and once he sent my sister and me off in the dinghy to practice capsizing it. Trying to capsize a dinghy on purpose was terrifying, especially with a crowd gathering expectantly on the bank while Dad was in the rubber blow-up boat shouting instructions. Your head goes into survival mode and wants to keep the dinghy upright. Dad was adventurous and he let us have fun but he'd always have his health and safety hat on too. Preparations could take an age, as everything was checked and double-checked and all the necessary safety measures were always in place. I knew Dad would never put us in danger so if he told me something was safe, I trusted him implicitly. I never ever questioned him.

Dad and my sister were close in a different way. She shared Dad's obsessive gene and was also highly academic, intelligent and dedicated. She was outgoing and more of a risk-taker than me so they'd go climbing together or out for runs. But whereas my sister was more competent and confident than I was, I needed reassurance and that's when I'd turn to Dad. If I was rock-climbing, for example, he'd be beside me assuring me that I wouldn't fall and encouraging me to give it a go. I needed Dad to provide that feeling of safety.

My parents' marriage seemed rock-solid too. They were always kind and affectionate to each other and worked well as a team, and because they worked together they had a lot in common. I suppose I held their marriage up as an ideal and hoped that I'd find that kindness in someone too. I saw it in Nick the moment I met him, when I was just fourteen and he was fifteen, but sadly my parents were less enamoured. They felt we'd met too early and it led to a fractured relationship between the three of them.

My parents tolerated Nick but couldn't hide the fact that they wished I'd never gone out with him in the first place. Nick and I split for a while. We had met young and Nick needed to explore other options. He had started sixth form college and the temptation of other girls was calling him. At the back of my mind I always knew we would spend the rest of our lives together but when – I did not know the answer to that one. Occasionally our paths crossed at parties and then eventually we got back together. By that time Nick was a smoker and had failed his A-levels. He was very laid back and his personality seemed contrary to everything my parents believed in when it came to working hard, taking life seriously and looking after your body. Nick didn't need a risk assessment to have fun and that's what I liked about him. Of course my parents could have fun too but everything had to be controlled. They never really let their hair down and even at a family party, there was no loud music, dancing or a good flow of booze. My father told me once that he'd never experienced a hangover. This gives a valuable insight into his values and expectations.

My parents never shouted or ranted and raved. Everything was done quietly and arguments were frowned upon. If my dad lowered his voice and used a certain tone, then I knew I was in serious trouble. By the same token, if I was angry I wasn't allowed to shout which could leave me feeling utterly frustrated. As a result, there was a lot of tension in our house so I'd escape to the house that Nick shared with his parents. That caused a lot of resentment between me and my parents but it felt easier at Nick's. At the time, I assumed the root of the problem was my relationship with Nick. It's only later that I realised that those were the years when Mum was secretly coming to terms with Dad's wish to transition into a woman.

Consequently, the dynamics in our house had shifted and I had no idea why. Mum had changed too, becoming more introverted and presenting a hard exterior which on occasion would lapse, but only for a short while. Because the atmosphere was increasingly difficult at home, I sought refuge with Nick.

After Dad told me the truth I felt like I'd lost the man I'd spent all those years loving. But he hadn't gone and that was the difficult thing. He was still there… but he wasn't. When Dad told me what was really going on in July 1987, he no longer looked exactly like my dad, but then again he wasn't like a woman either. By the time Dad revealed that he was transgender, he'd already had a nose job in 1980 and had his Adam's apple shaved down in 1988. He'd explained these surgeries away at the time by claiming that his nose and his Adam's apple were too big and, true to form, I hadn't questioned him. By then his beard had gone too – another physical marker of the man my dad had been. I remember Mum crying when Dad shaved off his beard and now I understood why. Even now I find a neatly trimmed but full-bodied beard and a large Adam's apple attractive on a man because to me they symbolise masculinity.

Dad had begun to look different, act different and sound different; his naturally deep voice was being strained as he was training his voice to be more feminine. He had new hobbies and a new friendship network. Soon he was surrounded by people who weren't men anymore but they didn't look like women either. I found it difficult to reconcile all of this in my head.

I wasn't given the time or space to grieve for the father I'd lost. Instead I was given a timeline of when the next changes were going to happen. Never mind that I didn't want them to happen at all. I couldn't question my father or argue because that would have meant raised voices, which weren't allowed in our house. Instead my feelings had to be controlled. I could only cry when I was with Nick or when I was alone. The only person who experienced any relief from the encounter was Dad. Carrying his secret had obviously been a huge burden for him and now it was to be ours.

My sister and I avoided the subject but also didn't spend much time together. We were both busy trying to live our lives as normally as we could. Mum wouldn't talk to us about it either. If we tried to raise the subject or ask her how she was coping, she'd tell us she didn't want us worrying about her and that she'd be ok. Only once did Mum confide in us that she was considering separating from Dad. I believe she got as far as looking in estate agents' windows but she never followed the plan through. She was still young and if she wanted could easily have started a new relationship. Whether or not she would ever have let anyone else get close to her is impossible to say.

A few weeks after Dad's confession, our parents decided it was time for a family conference to decide what this new person would be called. As we sat around the dining room table in conference mode, all clutching our drinks, there was no question that my dad was going to be called Dad any longer.

"Your mum isn't happy about me being called Mum." We all looked at Mum. Neither my sister nor I would have felt comfortable with that anyway. That was her title, her role and hers alone.

"I like the name Joan."

"Why?"

"No special reason, I just like it."

However, we felt Joan needed something that marked him out as a close family member so Auntie Joan was created. It's only now that I'm able to see how that decision meant Dad slipped down the family hierarchy. My parents had always been equal, but now Dad was one rung lower than Mum when it came to parenting. Sadly, I could never bring myself to tell Dad how deeply it pained me to lose him or what a huge loss I'd suffered. I knew how much it would hurt him. I craved the cuddles from my dad, like when I was a little girl climbing onto his lap.

From then on whenever I came home I'd be unsure who was going to greet me. Each time I opened the front door I'd wonder if Dad was going to look like Dad or whether he would be dressed as Joan. The first time I saw my dad cross-dressed was a real shock. He was wearing a pleated, flowery skirt and a blouse and his hair had grown over his collar. He had dressed conservatively and was wearing minimal make-up but still, seeing Auntie Joan in the flesh made me feel really uncomfortable. Dad was dressed as a woman but he wasn't a woman. For several years I found it hard to look him in the eye and I didn't want any physical contact with him. We both sensed a barrier but I continued to give him hugs to help keep the feelings of unity, love and connectivity flowing. Yet I had to behave as though there was nothing unusual going on. In a way I became as adept at hiding my true feelings as my dad had been for all those years.

Eventually Dad's mannerisms changed too and started to become more natural. He had lots of speech therapy but on occasions it jarred to hear him speaking softly and then standing in a typically male pose. Some elements about him were very feminine such as the hair, clothes and make-up, while others weren't. At times when there was less care being taken his male stance, and the old dad clothes, would re-appear, for example when going out into the garden. This I found hugely confusing. I struggled to make sense of the relationship my sister and I had had with Dad throughout our childhoods and also the one he had with Mum. Had it all been a lie because he wasn't the person he wanted to be? Had Dad ever been in love with my mum or had it just been a big facade to cover up who he was? Did he really love us, and see us as a family, or was it all a total cover-up? It also made me question my own relationship. Was Nick suddenly going to tell me he was gay or transgender at some point in the future? I found myself questioning everything I thought I knew as normal.

By 1990 the tension in my parents' house was unbearable. Just like before there were no arguments, but the atmosphere felt very odd between them. Often, when Mum found things difficult, she'd seek comfort in slumberland. Retreating into her own space was how she coped. When Dad was living as Joan full-time, Mum often made excuses to miss family celebrations, purely because she couldn't face putting on a united front to a large number of people. My sister and I felt the same but we weren't able to protest. We kept our real feelings tied up so that we could project the fake sense that we were in control.

Mum didn't want Dad's new friends in the house, so in 1992 he bought a flat around the corner. In some ways it was as though they had separated, but they hadn't at all. I found it difficult to cope with and hated visiting Dad in his flat. Dad wanted to try and make it home but it only exasperated the difficulties even further. Luckily Dad's kindness, empathy and compassion transferred themselves to Joan and she remained an independent, practical person. Even so, the mountaineering, running, rock-climbing and sailing I'd always associated with my dad soon stopped. Joan still behaved the same towards me as my dad always had, but my nerves and self-consciousness meant that I put up a barrier between us by keeping the physical contact to a minimum and phoning instead if possible. Quite honestly I was embarrassed about Joan and with that came huge guilt. Guilt because deep down I knew I shouldn't feel that way.

It took a long time before I accepted that my dad and Joan were the same person, while some family members still struggle with this today.

However, as wonderful as Joan was, ultimately, she was not my dad – that is to say, the dad I had grown up with. I felt I had to be supportive and that I would be seen as disloyal if I wasn't understanding enough, but I found it difficult because quite simply I wished that Joan didn't exist. I understood that she needed to have the life she wanted, but I just wanted my dad back. So, while I had to be supportive, it was also the last thing I wanted to be. I felt very conflicted.

My normal had been changed because Dad was finally coming to terms with who he really was after forty years of battling with his normal. Other people's normal will be changed by separation, divorce, bereavement, illness or old age. Nevertheless, I had to change my perception of normal.

- How was I going to fix this breakdown of my normal?
- How does anyone fix their broken normal?
- Where was I going to start?
- What was my next move?

Life is complicated, a lot like chess. The rules seemed so complicated: you can only move this way or that way, but if you position yourself in this place in comparison to that one, you will be taken or put yourself into a checkmate situation. My life had suddenly become like a complicated and extremely slow chess game. You can tell this person but not that person. You can call me this but not that, because it doesn't link up with my vision of normal. Nothing slotted into place any longer. It was rather like being given a box with a 500-piece jigsaw, but after hours and hours of working on it you realise that every piece is from a different jigsaw.

So what do you do?

Do you chuck it all in the bin, do you struggle to adapt, or do you become malleable so that you can retrieve some semblance of a normal life again?

" **What lies behind you and what lies in front of you pales in comparison to what lies inside of you.** "

Ralph Waldo Emerson, mid 19th century American essayist, lecturer and poet

The mother I kept

My mother – a kind and loving person who sometimes found it difficult to really let her feelings flow – was a dedicated mother, wife and teacher. Mum did most of the parenting and organised the housework, alongside running a busy career. Teachers are never able to greet their own children from school at 3pm but she always ensured there was someone welcoming to meet us at the front door. Mum was enormously capable at many practical skills and she excelled in dressmaking, knitting and making the most of the fresh fruit grown in our large garden. My mum is renowned for her stewed fruit of all varieties. Through her guidance I learnt my dressmaking skills and how to blanch vegetables and create fruit puddings.

I was a home bird, and often suffered from earache and tonsillitis. Before I started full-time school I relished the time I was able to spend with my mum listening to *Listen With Mother* on the radio, or watching *Jackanory*, *Paddington Bear*, *The Magic Roundabout* and *Play Away*. As my sister and I got older the three of us would watch *Blue Peter*, *Ask The Family*, and dance, prance and air guitar to *Top of the Pops*. My sister and I relished our bedtime stories. Mum would sit on our beds while she read. I remember on occasions that I would have to wake her up so I could snuggle under my covers and get my goodnight kiss. My sister and I shared a bedroom until well into our teens which meant great competitions: who could touch the ceiling as we bounced on our beds and used our mattresses as a landing ground for somersaults, or who could get dressed the quickest under the covers.

Our homework was always done at the kitchen table while Mum prepared our evening meal. With Dad often coming in late after meetings, it was a quick tea and a short amount of quality time to snuggle up before it was time to sleep. Sometimes I'd lie in bed, listening to the reassuring sounds of the TV or the murmur of their conversations from the kitchen below, and I would feel that everything was alright with my world now that both Mum and Dad were home.

" Like pebbles on a beach
Kicked around, displaced by feet
Oh, like broken stones
They're all trying to get home. "

Broken Stones written by Paul Weller

Tying the knot – how would Joan walk her daughter down the aisle?

Life got back to some kind of normal, or rather, we muddled along as most families do. We all started to be able to get on with our lives without the constant niggling thoughts of how our lives had changed with the courage of my dad telling us his darkest secret. My parents had come to accept Nick more easily; he was working hard and had accepted the new dimensions of our family more easily than I had.

It had got to the stage in my life that I wanted to have a baby. This had been niggling at me for a while, but for me a baby meant marriage first and I knew that Nick wasn't going to pop the big question any time soon. After knowing each other for thirteen years, he hadn't asked me so far and we had never discussed it, so the betting was that he was never going to ask me. I didn't want my future to just feature me, Nick and our dog, so one day I took the bull by the horns and asked him instead. *Hmm.* Not the response I was after, but I gave him some time to think about it. Luckily, he reluctantly said yes. In Nick's view we were committed to each other, we had a mortgage and a dog so in his eyes, why was getting married going to make any difference? The difference was in me. I wanted a baby but I also wanted to be married with my baby.

Nick, being Nick, didn't want a lot of fuss. The next big question for me was: who was going to give me away? My sister had had the honour of being walked down the aisle by my dad, but he was now living full-time as a woman, as Joan. Joan had undergone her orchidectomy (removal of the testes) and penectomy (removal of the penis) in 1991. Joan was now working towards her main transformational operation of the vaginoplasty, urethroplasty, clitoroplasty and labiaplasty (development of the vagina, urethra, clitoris and labia) in 1993.

Nick and I had decided that there was no point in an engagement; we'd known each other long enough, and we had been living together for a couple of years, so we might as well just get on with it. Six months tops until the big day.

With no dad to give me away, I hadn't really got the dream wedding I'd had in mind, of my family and friends happily together.

Nick was saying, "If there's too many people there I'm not going!"

My mum was saying, "If you and Nick want to just go off and get married, I totally understand. We will give you the money to do it."

My mother-in-law was saying, "If you just go off and get married and I'm not given the opportunity to come to your wedding, I'll never speak to you again!"

Since our new family unit had been introduced to my in-laws, a deeper respect and understanding had developed between them and my parents. A respect regarding differences between individuals and situations, and trying to manage the best that we could under the circumstances in the way we were living our lives. When you think about it, how many weddings don't have a struggle and battle of wills over arrangements, and often lifelong fall-outs, between extended families? I didn't want that. Our family had already changed beyond recognition, so going off and getting married on our own was not an option, even though Nick and I actually quite liked that idea. The first place to start was finding out what Nick wanted, but I wasn't expecting such a long exclusion list. No fuss. Not too many people, fourteen at the most. No official photographs. No official cake. No church. No cars. It upset me to think that Nick didn't want to show off our celebration of unity but I wasn't going to argue with his restrictions because I wanted to keep my eye on the main objective.

My dad? "It's your choice Cath."

We were stripping this wedding down to the bare bones: thirteen and a half people, the half being my six-month-old nephew. Even though Dad's main operation was looming, he was unable and not willing to change his outward appearance. I could understand that, especially given the timeline of his forth-coming major operation, and I wouldn't have expected him to do it, even though Mum would have liked it. That would have made the whole scenario even more... weird. Still, he wasn't my dad as I knew him any longer; he was Joan – and yet, still only family and my in-laws knew the truth.

None of my friends knew, partly because I hadn't really kept in touch with them. My old friends were there in the background but nothing had forced my hand into having to tell them. And I hadn't yet developed enough trust to tell my new friends, even though I liked and respected them. What would they say if I told them? I had laughed when Dad told me – what might they do? While I was able to keep Dad's new identity separate, my mother had had to manage this conundrum every day of the week, living and working in the same area. A respected member of the neighbourhood and the local teaching community was everyone's business.

Some of their friends had already faded away, and Mum had also coped with the varying reactions from our neighbours, her work colleagues, the pupils, their parents and the press. A parent had spotted my dad as Joan out and had informed the local newspaper. The last thing my mum needed was the press knocking on the front door, waiting at her workplace and spying through the windows, making sneaky phone calls and trying to prise information from anyone who answered, but that is exactly what happened to us. For a few days it was exactly like you see it on the telly at our house: the curtains drawn, our family moving through a gang of press, letting the phone ring and not talking to anyone about anything. The reporters making sneaky phone calls to the workplace hoping to chat up a member of staff who was willing to reveal all.

You might be reading this thinking, surely this is exactly when you need your friends? But this was the early 1990s, and most transsexuals were keeping their secret under wraps and not making the brave decision to follow through with the transformation to their real identity. How did you know who to trust? Some people had to be told because they were our extended family, or because Mum and Dad had to live and work with them on a daily basis, but who could you trust with your deepest and darkest thoughts around this subject?

What was going on in my headspace was still a struggle that I had to engage with alone. There was no offer of support for me, my sister and close family members. Nobody came along and said, "Hey Cath, this must be really hard for you, do you want someone to talk to about it? You know, to help you work out the confusion that must be going on in your head?" To be honest, I didn't think to ask for it either; I thought I should be able to work this out for myself and at the time it wasn't as acceptable to go for counselling as it is now. I thought that I always had to show support and that I was being a bad daughter if I felt conflicted in any way.

My mum was able to seek support and had been doing so for a long time. Confiding in her counsellor several times a week helped to keep her feeling sane. My dad sought his support through his doctors, the consultants and, eventually, networking with other transsexuals at the hairdresser's and each other's homes. However, I, my sister, plus my grandparents and extended family only really had my mum to ask questions of; and that was difficult as she was too close to him and we could see she was struggling herself. It was a challenging situation and I don't think that my dad really understood how many of us truly felt because none of us were able to express it. He had spent fifty years struggling with being in the wrong body and his own terrible angst – so who were we to voice our unhappiness? What I really struggled with was the fact that I had known this person for the past twenty-three years as a man, with a beard, who sailed, who walked the mountains, who rock-climbed and, when he was a young man, had the strength to lift a garden roller over a fence for the neighbour. To suddenly find out that my dad wanted to be a woman was a huge blow to my whole belief system.

So to wonder if I wanted my dad at my wedding was a difficult question to answer. I felt that he wasn't here anymore.

How well did I know Joan?

Should I ask my uncle to give me away instead?

Which one? (I had four.)

Given that Nick wanted a small wedding, if I asked one uncle, then all the uncles and aunties would have to come to a pointless wedding where there would be no bridegroom.

Should I ask my mum to give me away? Now I wish that I had pursued this option further.

The only close male friend I had was to be the best man, so that was not an option.

Should I marry without Dad, perhaps?

So, on 30 July 1992, off we went to the registry office together, with the best man driving us and we walked down the aisle together. I had eventually found the compromise. Joan came to the restaurant after the marriage ceremony. Even though it was unspoken, I think that everyone felt uncomfortable about my dad not being present. Even though it didn't feel right at the time, we still had a nice day and Nick and I were now married. In fact, there was another wedding party at the restaurant with us which had the big church ceremony going on with the official photographer, seating plan, big white dress, big iced cake, the whole family present. And you know what, the bride and bride-groom were arguing so much at the table that one of their guests, in passing, jokingly said, "Can I come and join your party? You all look as if you are having a lovely time."

It just goes to show that appearances can deceive. Who knows what is really going on under the surface?

> 1 + 1 definitely = 2 for
> Nick and I at least.

The high divorce rate, the ups and downs of marriage and the pressure to have the perfect life can be very demanding for most people. How do you know when to stay together and when to call it a day? For Mum, she must have wondered how real their marriage was, and whether life would be better for her alone. How many times these thoughts must have run through my mum's head I'll never know. It upsets me to think of the heartache she must have endured, that the man she married was not who she thought he was. She must have felt cheated but then she also agreed that my dad should have his operations, demonstrating her loyalty to him. My mum was not one to show us her true feelings; she felt she was there to parent, not to share her own worries. She would say: "You are my children and I look after you. I do not give you cause for concern over me." Admirable? Yes. Hard for us too though? Yes. On the odd occasion, it was a relief to see Mum at her most sensitive, when she was able to share a snippet of her deepest thoughts. The thought of waking up in the morning and sitting eating her breakfast on her own was not an appealing option. So she didn't leave. Instead, she demonstrated her values. Her marriage vows were for life and she was going to abide by them.

" Gender dysphoria is a condition where a person experiences discomfort or distress because there's a mismatch between their biological sex and gender identity. It's sometimes known as gender identity disorder (GID), gender incongruence or transgenderism.[1] "

All the stuff I never knew

As a family we muddled through. Every few years my dad made alterations to himself without us really understanding why. The next phase of surgeries and treatments comprised of:

- Vaginoplasty, urethoplasty, cliteroplasty and labiaplasty surgery in 1993
- Prolapse surgery in 1995
- Breast augmentation in 1997
- Electrolysis to remove facial hair once a week for eight years.

Gender dysphoria is now a recognised condition. In December 2002, the British Lord Chancellor's office published a Government Policy Concerning Transsexual People document that categorically states, "What transsexualism is not... It is not a mental illness" but it comes at a huge cost. The options are either long waiting lists in the NHS or paying between £10,000 and £29,000, depending on how many procedures are required.

To help me with the writing of this book I had the honour of interviewing an excellent general surgeon, who sub-specialised in gender reassignment surgery between 1993 and 2011. He explained that it is very difficult to determine whether someone has gender dysphoria. Nobody really knows why it happens. Is it nature and the exposure of hormones to the brain when the embryo is only a few weeks old, or is it nurture? There is no diagnostic test, no blood test or genetic testing, therefore all safe diagnosis decisions to operate are determined by the client's history of their thought processes and patterns of feelings. This is why it is so important for people who are requesting gender reassignment to undertake the two-year real-life test in their chosen gender. This test is not only to live as their desired gender but also to:

- Begin the hormonal changes
- Take time to realise what it entails being the opposite gender
- Understand what they have to give up
- Begin to establish their new way of life
- Have time to consider their family relationships, because the majority of families find it very difficult to cope
- Become emotionally stable
- Establish their new sexual role.

He stated, "There is a lot at risk not only to themselves but also to the relationships with their families. The gender reassigned group are one of the most grateful groups of patients, because they have been through so much struggle already before getting to the stage of talking to health professionals. Once the hormonal treatment has begun there is no going back for those going from female to male. After six months of hormones, the new husky voice and facial hair will remain after the hormones are no longer taken. Going from male to female is not so much of a one-way street because the client's oestrogen levels will need to be retained for the rest of their life. The good news for those going from male to female is the oestrogen will make the prostate shrink, reducing the risk of prostate cancer until the prostate is removed."

The default gender of a foetus in the womb is female because the womb is awash with female hormones[2]. The introduction of the sex hormone, androgen, can affect the brain at six to nine weeks in the womb, depending on the level and how responsive the mother's response system is. As far as Joan is concerned, the imbalance occurred while my grandma was carrying my dad. It was a mix-up, nothing to do with what she had eaten or her emotional wellbeing at the time. Our bodies are complicated systems and our development depends on a whole succession of processes that have to link up accurately or else the body goes into a confused state. Our biological sex is determined by the physical development of the sex hormones and the presence or lack of the testes gene in the Y chromosome. Confusion occurs if the hormones or genes aren't functioning correctly, and aren't released into the foetus at the right time in its development. No wonder the mind, body and soul sometimes have a massive argument between themselves, almost coming to blows at times. It is nature not nurture that determines someone's gender identity.

When you look at the figures it is astounding how many people are born into the wrong bodies. A survey of 10,000 people undertaken in 2012 by the Equality and Human Rights Commission found that 1% of the population surveyed was gender variant, to some extent. While gender dysphoria appears to be rare, the number of people being diagnosed with the condition is increasing, due to growing public awareness. However, many people with gender dysphoria still face prejudice and misunderstanding.[3]

To put it very simply:

- 1 in 10,000 men are born a transsexual
- 1 in 30,000 women are born a transsexual

This is according to the UK Trans Info site.[4]

Patients under care in the UK   = 9,617
People on the waiting list in the UK   = 5,057
Total   = 14,674

The total UK population in 2015 was 64,715,000 people[5], meaning that approximately 0.022% of the population in 2015 were struggling with their identity issues. This may be a minuscule percentage, but like anything, the more you focus on an issue, the more you see and hear about it.

To develop a clearer understanding of how changing from one gender to another affects others in the workplace, I spoke to Dad's old manager, Bip.

We started the conversation off at the time Bip learned about my dad's gender dysphoria. "In 1980 your dad had been poorly and as this was a rare occasion for him to be off work I decided to visit your dad at home." Like us, Bip had always wondered why my dad had undergone operations such as a nose job and the shaving of his Adam's apple at his time in life, but like the rest of us never really questioned it any further.

The thing was, back then, there was no safety around discrimination for transsexuals so having to manage the workplace with this news was always going to be a hot potato for everyone. Dad had spent so many years practising not being the person he truly wanted to be that he had become an expert at covering it up. When the staff were informed about his intention to transition, it was a shock for everyone. The junior members of staff were worried about Joan being seen out in public but there was actually never any comeback besides one parent who immediately informed the press. In fact, Bip thinks that some staff may even have passed Joan in the streets without realising it. Bip went on to explain that staff soon got used to it and only one junior member of staff really felt he could not manage this particular situation and decided to leave. Other people in the profession would ask after my dad out of curiosity and to check that the rumours were true. When parents tried to wheedle information from other members of staff it was quickly explained to them that this was not the nature of the meeting.

Dad was very lucky to be working with people who were mainly extremely understanding and flexible in their outlook in life. Unfortunately, others haven't been so fortunate and have been attacked in the street and experienced emotional, verbal and physical abuse in the workplace.

The advice that Bip would give to anyone with gender dysphoria is to "talk to their manager as soon as possible". This allows the company or organisation to start planning for any changes that would need to be made in order to ensure the smooth running of the business. It would give everyone time to get used to the shock, the new name and changes in the person's appearance, or to get used to a new member of staff if the person intended to leave. Bip also felt very strongly about the impact on that individual's work performance. The secrecy of holding onto something so important would have an impact on sleep patterns, concentration levels and maybe on decision-making skills, possibly creating a long line of unintentional consequences. As a close working colleague, manager and friend Bip knew he needed to:

- Be supportive
- Be honest
- Listen and ask questions
- Iron out any disputes as quickly and as efficiently as possible.

Life as a manager is now easier with more detailed, LGBT-friendly employment laws in place, but then Bip needed to set up a protocol and act if necessary to protect the person in the minority. Thankfully he never had to put this into practice to support Joan.

On a personal level, the change to Joan never affected their relationship but for Bip, like me, it took a while to get used to the name change. The stumbling over the mix-up of name and gender is confusing and can riddle people with guilt. Work colleagues, like family members, will be struggling with a whole host of questions but may be afraid to ask with so much emphasis on political correctness.

"

Yesterday a child came out to wonder
Caught a dragonfly inside a jar
Fearful when the sky
was full of thunder
And tearful at the falling of a star
And the seasons they go
round and round
And the painted ponies
go up and down
We're captive on the carousel of time
We can't return we can
only look behind
From where we came.

"

The Circle Game written by Joni Mitchell

The new addition

It was 1994 and I was pregnant with my first child. Nick and I were both over-joyed and ready for the new challenge that was about to take over our lives. My mum and Joan were overjoyed but it was not their first grandchild so it was all being taken in their stride. The difference being this one would be in England and not the other side of the world where my sister and family were now living.

> 1 + 1 now = 3 and ½,
> the ½ being the dog.
> Almost near perfect.

My husband proudly stated, "This baby isn't going to change our lives." Anyone with any common sense knows that babies always change lives. The responsibility, for a start. Then there are the night feeds, nappy-changing, getting into a routine, the bottles, the crying and the not knowing whether you are doing it all right. I don't think he had thought that statement through very carefully.

As soon as you know you are pregnant, especially with your first, it is all you can think about. Being pregnant consumes your whole life, from morning sickness, finding the right clothes to fit, recording the movements, going to clinics, worrying about if your baby is going to be perfect, birthing plans (in my opinion a waste of time), buying the right equipment, to being frightened of actually giving birth and packing your overnight bag. I'm breathless just thinking about it. When the actual labour comes, it feels like all hell is let loose and you just want the baby out as quickly as possible. And to top it all, we moved house two weeks into parenthood.

Nevertheless, it was good to have something else other than Dad and his transition to occupy my mind instead of wondering who knew, who didn't know, and how was I going to refer to my parents from now on. Do I refer to Mum and Dad, my mum and my Auntie Joan, or my parents? There was also the concern about people asking what had happened to my dad, and why was my Auntie Joan such a large part of my life? Were my parents divorced, was my dad dead or had he moved away? Joan was now a convincing female and was a lot more relaxed about living her life as a woman. However, there would be the question regarding all our relationships to one another. Was Auntie Joan my mum's sister or sister-in-law, my dad's sister or was she married to his brother? None of us knew the answers to these questions when we discussed it. Well, actually I tell a lie: my dad knew what he wanted to be called as he had always dreamed of being a mother, but my mum, understandably, wasn't going to agree to that. That was her role and only hers to have. Looking back at it, none of us were brutally honest to my dad, and it would have felt brutal to have been that honest. My mum, my sister and I still didn't want this to be happening, but the process had gone so far now we had to find our way through it, to try to accept, understand, adjust and get on with life the best that we could. We had to find our new normal again.

To alleviate all the questions, it was easiest to keep people at arm's length. The questions wouldn't come up because I wouldn't let people get close enough to me to ask the questions in the first place. There, a solution. Time to relax the mind for a bit.

Undergoing transgender reassignment is not an easy, cheap or pain-free process for anyone. The individuals have to have nerves of steel to keep going, managing the emotional and physical pain to get to being their true self, and dealing with the upheaval of almost starting again and trying to make the new life live up to the dream. Joan never wobbled from her goal to become Joan. She was never deterred by the setbacks, or the pain and discomfort.

The repercussions of my dad's gender reassignment were wide, varied and never-ending. My children were never going to have two granddads. They were going to have a grandma and a nan but only one granddad and an Auntie

Joan who really wanted to be a grandma as well. My grandparents and my uncles were, I can only assume, introduced to the big dream of their son and brother in a similar vein to myself. Who knows what they went through and felt and how they explained it to those close to them? Dad's transition was never openly discussed in our extended family. You might hear snippets, or whispers, or spot an awkward glance or conversation now and again though. Like me, my uncle John suspected that his brother must have a serious illness. He was preparing himself for the worst, so was almost relieved to find out that his brother's health was good and he *only* wanted to change sex.

My grandfather accepted it more easily than we imagined he would. He had an uncle who cross-dressed and eventually took his own life, presumably because he couldn't manage the everyday struggle that he had to face. So it was poignant that, out of everyone in our family, he was the most understanding of them all. This must have been a massive relief to Dad, to know that his parents would support him. Dad must also have felt sadness that there were so many wasted years of not being the person he really wanted to be, when actually it would have been OK to be more open. At first, my grandmother, like any great mother, worried that she had done something wrong when pregnant or perhaps it was how she had parented her son. She mithered over that for a while but soon came to the conclusion that having reared four boys she would now have the daughter she had always wanted. Even though Joan didn't hear this directly, the support and information received from her cousin made her feel at home and even more connected to her mother.

January 1995 came around and the whole family was on tenterhooks waiting for our first baby. The hospital bag had been packed, and the baby was clearly determined to stick it out before deciding to emerge into the big wide world. Meanwhile we were getting ready to move house, and Nick's nan had died days before my due date.

The labour started as a shambles. Nick was at a football match and of course there were no mobile phones at the ready for THE CALL. As my waters broke while I was cooking chilli con carne, it was my mum I rang. Thank goodness she soon tracked down this baby's father with the help of my mother-in-law. In the early hours of the morning, with a lot of pushing and lot of tugging with the forceps, our daughter was born. Oh, she was so gorgeous, perfect in every way, small, wrinkly, pink, no hair, and she kept me awake all night crying unless I held her tight. It was as if she didn't want me to let her go, now that she was in this big wide world of ours.

The doting husband arrived with flowers; I have never received so many from him before. As I watched him hold his daughter I could tell that he didn't care anymore that this baby was going to change our lives forever. Then my mum arrived with flowers, my sister-in-law arrived with flowers, my mother and father-in-law arrived with flowers… but still no Dad. As they left I couldn't be seen for flowers as they made a protective and beautiful screen from the world. It was fabulous, except for the one thing that was lurking at the back of my mind. I now had an important phone call to make. My dad, no, Auntie Joan, was also in hospital. There had been some complications with her operations that meant she would need some more surgery.

Why was I so scared to call? I now had a child to protect and nurture the best I could. How much did I even want Auntie Joan to be a part of my daughter's life? I suppose I was frightened of the complications it might have for us as a family. How was it going to affect my mum and Joan? Would there be an unspoken competition between them in terms of grandparenting because of the change in their roles in life? At the end of the day even though Joan would be called Auntie she would still be a grandparent. But I also knew without a shadow of a doubt she would be in totally capable hands with either of them. They would both love her, nurture her and always have her best interests at heart. As I studied my daughter's tiny face, I wondered how was I going to tell her about her grandpa when the time came?

Having left my daughter in the experienced hands of the ward staff, I dialled the number with no idea how I was going to introduce myself. Do I say I am the daughter of my dad, or the daughter of Joan Mason?

Too late, the receiver had been picked up and I heard a kind male voice stating his position in the world of science.

Another couple of seconds to gather my thoughts while popping the coins in the slot, but there was no going back now.

"Hello. I am… eh… Joan Mason's… eh… daughter," I said. "Please could you let her know that I have given birth to a daughter." Short, to the point and then I can return to the new joy in my life.

"Ah, hello, yes of course but she is just with me now, would you like to speak to her yourself?"

I wasn't expecting that. Not as simple as I thought.

"Yes. No… yes… please."

A very quick exchange of information with many uncomfortable pauses and, I hasten to say, I was not very forthcoming. Thankfully, our time to talk was soon up as the pips started sounding. I imagine that when the call ended Auntie Joan was close to, if not in, tears. I returned to my daughter with the arguments starting in my head all over again. Why does life have to be so hard, so complicated? You are such a bad daughter for complaining about your lot. You know that Dad, oh hell, Auntie Joan, will be great for your daughter. But how do I tell my daughter, and when do I tell her? How should I know?

All this was racing through my mind as I looked intently at my daughter's face with her eyes squeezed tightly shut as if trying to keep the light out. As I tickled her tiny fingers, she folded them around mine and I felt calmer. Despite everything, this was good. Nick was right: he and I had made a beautiful baby.

" Now is the only time that matters
And if you are unhappy
with life change it.
Life is too short
You are in control of your
own life and destiny. "

Linda Ellis, speaker and poet, from her book, *The Dash*

Kids, I have something to tell you...

I'm not sure if Nick and I ever sat down and discussed formally how to one day tell the children about Joan. In the end, it happened naturally when our two were nine and eight. But I have to say, this discussion had been on my mind since the day my daughter was born in 1995. *One day she'd have to know our secret.*

We didn't talk about Dad's gender dysphoria outside of the family but it continued to weigh heavily. Then I made a new friend and got my chance to tell someone outside of the family – and to try out how I would say it, to test the reaction. Instinct and karma led me to the long-limbed, dark-haired woman with the welcoming smile at the post-natal group I attended with my tiny daughter. A deep and lifelong friendship with Anne began. As we grew as mothers, our daughters grew, with the addition of brothers born in 1996 with only a couple of months between them. Since leaving school at sixteen, I had always kept a very small but close group of friendships. I had been quite happy to keep people at a distance. After all I was told to keep the family secret; nobody had said anything different, and this was the best way to do it, by keeping people at arm's length, until now. Anne was different. We had our children to keep us together, and they played, argued and slept in each other's beds regularly while we chatted, complained and laughed about our children, our husbands and occasionally our parents. With Anne I began to feel safe, plus she was a nurse, so I figured she would be more understanding than other people.

As in most relationships, I started to test the trust side of our relationship with little snippets of information and thoughts in search of Anne's reaction. At the beginning of our friendship, she worked on a women's plastic surgery ward mostly caring for people who had undergone breast implants and nose jobs. Looking for something more meaningful, she began her practice nurse training because she wanted to play a bigger part in supporting the community.

I was starting to need someone to confide in with whom I could discuss the ever-growing chatter in my head, which I had been able to keep under wraps for so long with the distraction of my children. The ban on keeping the family secret had never been verbally lifted but I needed to be able to talk to someone other than my family and Nick. I needed to have someone to go to when I finally told the children, in case it all went badly. Also, the children might want someone they trusted to talk about their Auntie Joan with.

Anne fitted the bill. There were a lot of similarities. We had been raised with similar values. We had one sister. We were loyal to our husbands. We got on well with a lot of people but only maintained a very small handful of what we would call 'close' friends. The time was coming nearer to confide in Anne and it was just a matter of when. And then the time happened.

As the children played and our husbands talked, we found ourselves standing in her kitchen together, Anne's back to me whilst she re-arranged the dirty crockery in the sink. I remember being so frightened about what to say, and how to say it. Although I felt safe with her, I had kept this information so secret that it had become a huge barrier to shift, like massive wooden doors that are so big and so heavy you need strong arms to push them open. I needed to find the right words in the right order to force the dead weight of the doors open, and just say it. Eventually, I began to explain. The pressure of wanting to speak out made my head hurt, my heart pound and my stomach screw up into a tight knot. There was no easy way to say this so I just had to take a deep breath and go for it. With her back to me I stammered,

"Anne?"

"Yes."

"There is something I really need to tell you."

"What's that?"

As Anne turned to face me and stood propped up against the kitchen sink with her long arms folded in front of her, I struggled to lift my gaze from the floor. "Auntie Joan is really my dad. I haven't said anything before because I have been too frightened."

I had finally said it. Anne, in a soft voice, simply said: *"Oh Cath."*

As she unfolded those arms and wrapped them around me, I cried. I cried out of relief. Someone else knew my secret. Not just my husband or another member of the family but someone I had chosen to tell. It was going to be okay with Anne because I had spent seven years building up a foundation of trust with her, and she had lived up to that trust. She had pulled through with her kindness, her caring, sensitive and compassionate nature. I knew she was going to be supportive. I just knew from the way she held and spoke to me. I had finally found the courage to tell someone, to start to break that vow of silence and secrecy. It felt amazing! It was the beginning of my recovery and my real acceptance of my new normal.

I had confided in and opened my heart to the right person. I had played a safe game plan that had worked out. It was the catalyst to sharing the burden with my children.

Shortly after this, we sat at the kitchen table like we did every meal time and the subject naturally turned to the family. I realised there was no better time to start the discussion.

My stomach started to churn at the prospect of telling them that the Auntie Joan who sometimes collected them from school and looked after them in the evenings wasn't who they thought she was. I looked to my children's dad for guidance but with him not being telepathic it was difficult to seek the unspoken support I needed.

"Kids, you have never enquired about why you have only one granddad. Do you not ever wonder about that?"

Puzzled, the kids looked at each other, mouths full of food, looking rather like hamsters. They shook their heads.

"Not really."

I could see I was just going to have to go for it.

"The reason I say this is because your Auntie Joan is really your other grandpa."

The eating stopped for a split second as they looked at me, then at their dad, who wasn't about to interrupt my flow, for a little confirmation, but his eyes were firmly fixed on his meal.

I could see I was going to have to get on with this on my own.

"Your Auntie Joan is my dad. Your Auntie Joan, way before you were born, decided he wanted to be the person he really wanted to be and that was a woman. My dad, who is now Auntie Joan, has had a change of sex. She has had the operations to change her from looking like a man to looking like a woman."

My children nodded. They carried on chewing in silence.

Were they not hearing me; was I imagining this, or were they not bothered?

"Do you understand what I am telling you?"

In unison and between mouthfuls, "Yep."

"What do you think about it?"

"Fine," they said. "Auntie Joan is Auntie Joan."

I exchanged glances with Nick as the burden I had been carrying for so many years seemed to lift from my shoulders.

I realised they hadn't known anything different.

All those years of worry about when, where and how to tell the children about their transgender grandpa were swept away in about two seconds. Auntie Joan was normal to them, end of story. I was almost envious. Why hadn't it been that simple for me?

When I looked back over my own childhood I was immediately drawn to our garden with its lawn, the garden that my sister and I and our friends had happily played in for the whole of our childhood. A large lawn that once housed a huge willow tree, which used to shed so many leaves in the autumn that it would take me and my sister a couple of days each autumn to rake up. Wheelbarrow after wheelbarrow loaded with leaves that we would transfer to the compost heap at the end of the garden.

The story of how Dad found the swing for our willow tree has always been a precious memory from my childhood. My grandparents, for as long as I could remember, had a caravan at Conway in North Wales. Our holidays and weekends away with them were always fun, walking on the beach with my grandma scouring for shells, while Grandpa played golf. After lunch, sitting on the grass outside with my sister, we would meticulously wash each shell, watching how their colours would change when wet and setting them out to admire and display for our grandma. The whole family would converge to walk on Conway Mountain where the bracken was taller than me. With my uncles and aunt we would dig holes on the beach and spend time in my uncle's canoe in the sea.

On one of these holidays, during one sunny warm evening, in the early 1970s, we were all walking on the beach when Dad spotted a gigantic rope with a knot at one end and a loop at the other, a washed-up anchor rope. The rope was soooo heavy, wet and laden with sand, but the excitement it created within our family was immense. It was obvious it was for securing a boat in the harbour because it had a loop to go over the mooring post and the knot to secure in the vessel. But where had it come from? What sort of vessel? How big a vessel? Dad's mind must have been working overtime because before I knew it the car was as near to the beach as possible and the rope was on the roof-rack ready for our journey home the next day. Everyone had got involved with transferring it onto the roof. Little did I know that this rope was going to play an important role in our childhood. Dad planned to hang it from our willow tree. The knot and the loop would hang down with a tyre jammed into the loop to make two swings. Wow, two swings!

I remember my dad putting the rope up into the willow tree on a dry day while my mum busied herself in the kitchen. I could see her going backwards and forwards, every so often looking out of the window to check on his progress. My sister and I were craning our necks, looking up into the dizzy heights of the leafed canopy, taking instructions and helping where we could. Being highly conscious of health and safety, my dad had attached himself to our monster of a willow tree with his rock-climbing harness, just in case. He wrapped the rope around one of the main branches of the tree with the knot, with the loop evenly positioned so we could reach both. This was a momentous day in our lives and brought a whole new meaning to our games in the garden.

At first, we struggled to get onto the knot so my dad would help us up until we managed the technique for ourselves. Once the tyre was in place in the loop we swung, swayed, climbed up, fell off, slipped down, getting rope burns on our hands, arms and thighs in our new adventure playground that Dad had made for us.

Over the years that followed, I would sit in the swing for hours with my rabbit, Honey, on my lap. She was a good listener, listening quietly while I ran my hand over her nose and ears and down her back as I poured out my concerns, my sadness and my anger, until I had shed all the emotion. She felt so beautiful and soft. I couldn't imagine, at that time, that one day there was to be no more Honey, no more rope swinging, no more willow tree and no more Dad.

> " I never knew that everything
> was falling through
> That everyone I knew was
> waiting on a cue
> To turn and run when all I
> needed was the truth. "

Over My Head (Cable Car) written by Isaac Slade and Joseph King

Didn't anyone ever tell you to put those feelings on a lead?

Before I start I feel I need to ask you a question:

Do you like to feel happy?

If you like to feel happy, how would you like to feel awesome?

I would love to feel awesome all of the time but I know that it is totally unrealistic. If we did we would become used to feeling awesome, and then it would feel ordinary. We would forget how great the feeling of being awesome used to be.

As we travel through our journey of life situations change, we grow up, our children develop and become independent and our ideas of how we should be living, thinking and what jobs we should be doing also change. In my own career my style of teaching has moved on. Long gone is the teaching of general art and design and in its place have come social and life skills where I feel I can support others in a more direct way and make a difference with a wider focus.

I think we can go through life easily losing track of how we are feeling. We are so busy just getting on with the day to day. I know I was: getting up early, walking the dogs, getting the kids ready for school, going to work, getting home, being with the kids and my husband, making sure everyone was happy, making sure the homework was done, doing household chores. Doing the best that I could do and losing track of what was actually going on inside myself. Although I was noticing a shift in my mind and body, like most people I ignored it, told myself I was being silly. What had I got to complain about? I had a job that I enjoyed, a great husband whom I loved, a couple of amazing kids, dogs, rabbits and good health.

Or so I thought. I had been noticing how tired I was all of the time; my lower back ached and it was so stiff that I was waking up at night with an uncomfortable neck. I altered my pillows and sure enough that helped for a while. But my body was now so stiff in the mornings that I had to roll out of bed. Is this what it was like to be forty? If this is how life was at forty, no wonder people complained about middle age. What was the rest of my life going to be like?

A trip to the doctor's and several trips to the physio didn't reveal anything, but a good click of the back eased the pressure and I continued as I had done before. Well, no. Actually I took some advice from my sister and I started to experiment with different exercises, altered my fitness regime so it was more varied and added in flexibility stretching which made a huge improvement. Then I carried on as usual: work, home life, making sure the kids had everything they needed, tending to my dogs and keeping an eye on the rest of the pets in our household, oh and not forgetting to get to the gym because you can only be perfect if you do all of that and have a good body shape as well.

1 + 1 doesn't = 2 any longer
but 2063 instead.

The new normal.

As I went about my daily life I noticed that my feelings were bouncing around more and more. I was struggling to get up in the morning to go to work, I was becoming moodier, and I so wanted to cry such a lot of the time. The kids would give me strange looks sometimes and I realised that I wasn't enjoying life much any longer.

Then one day in May 2007, I was walking up the car park towards my workplace, not feeling in love with my job or the world, when I saw someone I knew.

"Hi Judy, how are you?" I said.

My theory then was that if I got in first with the how are you's, I might get away with not having to lie about how I was really feeling in case it all came spilling out.

"I'm very well thank you," said Judy. "And Cath, how are you?"

This time my theory didn't work.

I found that I could not answer that very simple question. It was as if someone had got me in a strange contraption that was somehow crushing and stretching me into all sorts of strange shapes and swinging me around by the big toe. I can't describe how I felt; all I knew was that suddenly I felt wildly out of control and I didn't know what to do about it any longer. Standing there in that car park with Judy, I wanted to cry, I wanted to run away and hide, I wanted to laugh out loud until it went away and I also wanted to burst my bubble of secrecy and let all the emotion out once and for all.

When I think about it now, how many times have you been asked that "How are you?" question and you have said "Fine thanks" without even thinking about it or knowing that deep, deep down you feel at rock bottom, but at least there are some reserves just about keeping you afloat? This time I couldn't answer the question because I was in tears, trying to laugh the situation away. There were no reserves left for me to tap into. Judy put her hand on my arm and turned me around so she could take a look at me, and tried to make eye contact. I will never forget how Judy took control of the situation and how my future altered in that moment.

Don't things happen in strange ways?

I had got to the stage in my teaching career that I wanted to move but not upwards. Moving up into management and all that number crunching and doing jiggery-pokery with figures was not my idea of a fun time, so I was considering a sideways move into counselling. I like meeting people, I find them interesting; that is why I've taught for so long, and I enjoy helping them. But the funny thing was, later on when I was on sick leave with stress, my introductory course to counselling started at the same time as I was receiving counselling myself.

Counselling is great if you are someone who is prepared to open up and talk. Eventually I opened up and it all started to spill out. I started with something safe about my parents being disappointed with my O-level results and the struggle to keep my teachers happy, compared to my academic sister. After a couple of weeks when I started to feel more comfortable with the counsellor the real work started. Even in 2007 transgender was still a rare topic of conversation and to my surprise the counsellor was asking me all the wrong questions. This satisfied her curiosity rather than helping me find my answers. Her eyes lit up with excitement and her voice moved up a level to ask, "Do they still live together? Do they share a bed?"

Finding a professional person who could listen to me was the key to unlocking my unhappiness. My children were at the age where they were trying to develop their own values and personalities and it was fashionable not to listen to their mum. My husband was busy building up his business and was also coming to terms with both of his parents' ill health. I was in the middle of teaching a very emotionally demanding course fraught with safety complications that I felt weren't being acknowledged by the people around me at work. Being heard was the issue, but I wasn't even listening to myself.

What I love about my husband is how he can turn something serious into something light-hearted. One meal time around the kitchen table we were all coming to terms with me having counselling when Nick suddenly announced:

"Kids, by the time you are twenty-one you will be really screwed after we've infected you with all our baggage. Don't feel ashamed about going to counselling, everyone is doing it, it's normal. I think all babies should be born with a little label attached to their big toe giving them automatic access to ten hours of counselling."

This dramatic statement helped to turn my tears into laughter at just the right time. This laughter was infectious and flooded the room from wall to wall. I embarked on a realistic review of my life, of my feelings, and reminded myself that I couldn't change what had happened in the past. I couldn't change the fact that my dad wanted to be someone different. What I did know was that I could change how I felt about me. And I hated not feeling happy. I hated the fact that it was hard work having to put a happy face on when I felt so desperate inside. I hated that I wasn't being honest with myself about how I was really feeling. I was conning myself and the people I loved.

This is where my life coaching journey started. At first I thought this would answer all my prayers and I would be fixed. Just like that, rather like flicking a switch. Little did I know that on day one of my life coaching training I would be in tears. I had to think about what was important in my life, how everything slotted together. I had to think about my values and beliefs and more importantly the limiting beliefs I had been hanging onto. It was tough, and so many times I nearly headed for the door. But then the little voice inside my head would chirp up.

So keep running away and never sort out the crap that's going on inside your head.

How long are you going to keep this up? How many years have you been struggling for?

Oh, only about twenty.

Well, you can keep going on like this if you want to but it's a pretty shit life if you do, don't you think?

So I decided to accept the challenge and, as I developed my life coaching skills, I also developed a better understanding of myself. Human beings are funny creatures. We find excuses or distractions so that we don't have to face the really hard thoughts. Those uncomfortable feelings that are too difficult to tap into, that will ultimately make the biggest difference to us if we do.

My distraction was using my coaching skills in my teaching. Managing the difficult conversations about my parents didn't work for me any longer. My feelings were still going up and down rather like a noisy rollercoaster but now with a lower back pain in the sciatic nerve. Carrying on 'as normal' doesn't always work does it? My normal at the gym came to a halt as that muscle in my back finally decided it had had enough. I discovered what the phrase 'my back suddenly went' really felt like – excruciating pain and another week off sick.

For years I had been ignoring my body. Not in a destructive way through issues like substance abuse or having an eating disorder. I was abusing my body because it was throwing all sorts of symptoms at me that I was ignoring because I was too frightened to confront them. Experts didn't recognise the root cause and said there was nothing wrong with me. The truth was that I had spent too many years bottling up my feelings. I was keeping hold of a secret that was creating a huge conflict in my head that I rarely let out and only to people like Anne. Nick didn't really know what to do with me when I got like this; he didn't know what to say, and he didn't understand what was going on in my head because it was all in my head. If he had said: "Cath, what is the matter?" then probably it would have all come tumbling out. The problem was he didn't ask the magic question and so it never did. I was internalising my feelings so much that they were making me physically ill.

Our bodies tell us when enough is enough, but how often do we ignore the aches and pains? How often do we ignore the headache, the earache, and the stomach upset that is blamed on a virus, the changeable weather conditions or a bad curry? What is in our head seeps into our bodies without us even realising. Until of course we feel we need to find solutions to the aches and pains by taking painkillers and eventually going to see the doctor.

I was fed up of being a misery and I was determined to put it right. To make it easy for me to smile again and mean it. I was going to be the calm, bright and smiley person I had envied in others. I was going to deal with the burden of the secret that I'd been asked to carry so long ago, once and for all.

Finally, I had realised I had a choice as to how I wanted to feel and my choice was to change it.

Endnotes

1. www.nhs.uk/conditions/gender-dysphoria
2. http://healthdoctrine.com/hormones-factors-in-fetus-gender-and-child-future-development/
3. http://www.nhs.uk/conditions/gender-dysphoria/pages/introduction.aspx
4. https://uktrans.info/attachments/article/341/patientpopulation-oct15.pdf
5. http://www.populationpyramid.net/united-kingdom/2015/

PART TWO

7 steps to living your new normal

"

You do something to me
Somewhere deep inside
I'm hoping to get close to
A peace I cannot find
Dancing through the fire, yeah
Just to catch a flame
Just to get close enough
To you that
You do something to me
Something deep inside.

"

You Do Something to Me, written by Paul John Weller

Introduction to my 7 steps to living with my new normal

Call me a slow learner but having to face and live with my new normal was tough for me. I was in shock. I just didn't want to accept the change that had occurred and it took me twenty years to get to a place where I was ready to be really honest about my hurt and confusion, to understand and accept those feelings, and then come up with some strategies to help myself move forward.

When we go through big change, whether it is bereavement, redundancy, retirement, separation, any form of loss or trauma, there is a natural process. 'The Change Curve', as developed by the late Elisabeth Kübler-Ross, plots the changes that we naturally go through. My emotional development was no different to anyone else's, except we all emerge through the other side at different times depending on how long we choose to hold onto the feelings and emotions that we are experiencing. I say 'choose' because it is exactly that – a choice.

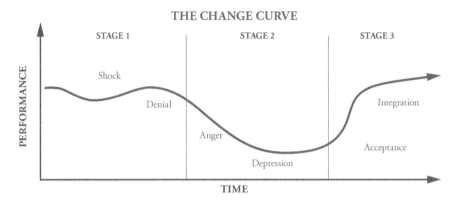

The "Change Curve" diagram is adapted from " The Five Stages of Death" from *ON DEATH AND DYING* by Elisabeth Kübler-Ross, Copyright ©1969 by The Elisabeth Kübler-Ross Family LP. Reprinted by arrangement with The Elisabeth Kübler-Ross Family LP and The Barbara Hogenson Agency. All rights reserved

Everything we decide to think, say or do, whether we are conscious of it or not, is our decision. For the majority of us, only 5% of our decisions come from our conscious mind. A pretty frightening fact, especially when you consider that we are having between 50,000 and 70,000 self-conversations a day, whether they are in the conscious mind or the subconscious. Therefore, 95% of the time we are unaware of why we are feeling, thinking and behaving the way we do. So much could go wrong and no wonder we can feel out of control sometimes. When you realise that, does it not make sense to learn more about ourselves and take back some control?

For twenty years I felt completely out of control. I was caught between stage one and two of the change curve. My head, heart and body were all disagreeing with one another, so no wonder I eventually came to a standstill. I just didn't know how to react any longer. There was so much confusion going on inside of me that eventually I came to a grinding halt with so much emotional baggage I didn't know what to do with anymore. The more I look back on it the more I realise that the back ache, the tiredness, the feverish feeling I got as I tried to manage everything was my body finally saying,

"Come on Cath, it's time. You can't go on like this any longer. You have been in denial, anger and depression over the transformation of your dad to Joan for too long. It's time to get your house in order."

In 2007 I took an introduction to counselling course, then my Life Coaching Diplomas and Neuro-Linguistic Programming. However, like so many other people, when you are working on your own personal development, you get so far and then you can easily get distracted because:

1. You start to feel a lot better.
2. You start to gain more control over your feelings.
3. You also get to the really difficult points so you go back to sweeping it under the carpet again.
4. The challenging conversations of keeping a secret continue.

I felt all of the above and distracted myself by using my newfound life coaching skills in my adult education career. It totally transformed it. I had already set up a Parent Craft course to support fathers in jail in developing their parenting skills, and was now setting up and teaching an Effective Thinking Skills course, both of which were well received. I learned how to use my voice, my facial expressions and my general communication skills to put my message across to these men more convincingly. It was really working… until the powers that be decided that they weren't going to fund the course any longer. As I threw my arms up in dismay I realised that this was the right time to consider my options. How was I really going to change my career and face my own issues going forward?

Career wise, I chose to give up my twenty-five years of adult education teaching experience with schools, colleges and prisons – and go it alone. I was going to combine my teaching and life coaching skills together without the confines of Ofsted, prison rules etc and start a new chapter.

So far, so good… However, I was aware that busying myself with imple-menting changes in my career was just me in denial, putting off the big acceptance and integration that needed to happen. Things came to a head in unlikely circumstances. It soon became apparent that my parents, now in their eighties, needed a little extra help at home, and I began spending more time with them, doing little jobs that they found stressful or tiring, such as sorting and shredding paperwork. So far, so normal… but funnily enough, it was this job, this coming together to burn through our past that brought things to a head. Doing the admin and paperwork meant facing practical issues such as: how exactly do I describe my relationship with these two women on paper? And from an emotional point of view, sitting down and sifting through meant more one-on-one time with Joan – and I enjoyed this. These quiet hours spent side by side working methodically in a companionable way helped me see her for her, and not a person who used to be my dad, perhaps for the first time in forty years. Did this mean I was moving closer to stage 3 of the curve, finally getting closer to that longed for acceptance and integration of Joan?

It did. One sunny spring day a few months into the task, I was up the garden burning a massive pile of forty years of paperwork. I was mesmerised by the way the cream paper turned yellow, curled and gradually the edges singed to ochre and then brown. There was something rather poetic about the movement and shapes of the flames, how they changed from yellow to orange with the occasional flash of green and blue. As I studied the depth of the red embers in the bottom I saw it. *Martin Homer.* Dad's signature on an old Mastercard paper receipt. My heart started to beat uncontrollably and my hands shook violently. I couldn't burn it! But I couldn't reach into the flames to grab it either. I frantically sifted through the rapidly reducing pile of papers in the box. A huge sigh of relief. There were more. Many more. Mum and Dad's signatures, neatly side by side on many documents, just as they had always been. I folded one of each and put them carefully and safely in my pocket. My heart stopped pounding but the reality of what had just happened struck me with huge force. I was burning my dad, I was finally letting him go, and with this thought I could feel the last twenty-five years of denial, anger, frustration and confusion rise up through my body and escape quietly through my tears and sobs. Eventually the sobs subsided and the heat from the flames left crusty salt streams down my cheeks as a calm embraced me, as if comforting me and saying, *"Cath, everything is going to be alright".* I had finally reached the third stage of the change curve – and allowed myself to let my dad go.

The amazing thing about our brains and the way the neurotransmitters work is that we can grow new connects but that isn't enough to make great change. We also have to unlearn the ones we already have. In Norman Doidge's book *The Brain That Changes Itself* he discusses the way this works, in terms of grieving for example:

"Though reality tells us our loved one is gone, 'its orders cannot be obeyed at once.' We grieve by calling up one memory at a time, reliving it, and then letting it go."

In other words, we turn on each neural network that we originally wired up, then we have to relive it for us to be able to let it go and say goodbye. This is also going to be the same for parents who are experiencing empty nesting syndrome, retirement, redundancy and many other forms of major change.

Almost within hours of finding Dad's last signatures and letting go, life started to come together. A true eureka moment. Now I understood **why** I was doing so much to teach and support others and how they could work for **me**. As a teacher and a life coach, I had got my strategies to support myself and others but I now finally understood how they linked together and how I have used them. That could only make me a better coach and teacher as well as a happier person. For the first time in years, I felt a deep sense of peace and excitement.

With this in mind, I would like to share with you my '7 steps to living your new normal'.

By following these seven steps you will be able to see more clearly and find your deep sense of peace and excitement. However, there is no black and white to managing your change because there are so many variables, such as:

- Your own belief systems
- Your values in life
- Results of positive and negative past experiences
- Your levels of self-honesty
- Reactions from others
- Your own natural levels of optimism and pessimism
- Your support structures
- The enthusiasm for your commitment levels and willingness to change

It is, however, important to remember that with these strategies, there is an order to them. You might find you keep going backwards and forwards, re-addressing and checking that you are progressing in the right direction. Always remember that there is no right way, only the right way for you.

If you want to address your 'living with normal' follow the strategies, use them fluidly and keep going back to the previous strategies if you need more clarification. This book is to be used as an exercise book. Don't be frightened to write in it, highlight areas, doodle in the corners when you are thinking. Some of the most useful books I have read have the corners of the pages turned over, notes in the margins and highlighted text. I know then I can go back to it and find what I am looking for easily.

> " Trust yourself.
> You know more than
> You think you do. "

Benjamin Spock, American paediatrician, author of *Baby and Child Care*

Strategy 1:
The importance of our values

Values are what matters to us. They are our rule book for life. If we are ever unsure about a decision we need to make, we usually go back to our values and ask – what really matters? The answer helps us take the right path.

Our values initially come from how we are brought up, by our parents, other caregivers and other people in authority such as teachers. However, as we get older we start to find our own values in life by listening and viewing how others live their lives and the emotions that are created within us when we are in different situations.

There are two sorts of values: core values and secondary values. Core values are what we get from secondary values, for example:

Secondary Value	Core Value
Relationships	Love, affection, trust, respect, truth, honesty, kindness, understanding, confidence, confidentiality, authenticity
Work	Money, respect, credibility, trust, confidence
Holidays	Excitement, relaxation, adventure, learning
Money	Freedom, enjoyment, relaxation, excitement

However, these values will change over time depending on where we are in our life, our relationships with others, our work, our confidence levels and our health.

An example of a destructive relationship and love

It may be that you were brought up with very loving parents who showed affection easily and had a healthy trust between them so love would be a main core value. However, as you grew up you may have got into a relationship which you put a lot of love and trust into but the relationship became destructive in some way. Perhaps the other person in the relationship found it hard to develop trust which led to manipulation to enforce love. This might then have swayed the importance of love as a core value because of the way that love was shown to you. Therefore, the word love would create doubt in your mind and make you feel as if you were undeserving of it. Some people are able to break away from this sort of relationship because they can see within themselves how they want their life to be. Others may decide to stay in that destructive relationship or go from one destructive relationship to another because they may think that is the way their life is meant to be. It has become their new normal.

In contrast, a lot of parents really struggle when their children flee the nest and move away from the bosom of nurturing and comfort that parents want to give them. As parents, we should be happy that they are making their own way in the world and enjoy seeing their new adventure unfold. When women give birth the bond between mother and child is enhanced by the injection of the hormone oxytocin, a neuromodulator which enhances the synaptic connections to bring about real change, during labour and breastfeeding. The evidence suggests that this injection of oxytocin helps support our devotion to our children. However, this bond can be difficult to release.

How do you break the cycle and start discovering your core values in life?

How do you make the bond easier to release when your child leaves home?

I learnt a great little exercise along my coaching career that I would like to share with you.

YOUR SELF HELP SECTION

Write down five things that are important to you. Try and keep it to core values but don't worry about the order of importance at this time.

e.g.

1. Money

2. Love

3. Trust

4. Respect

5. Adventure

1. Your Values:

1. _____

2. _____

3. _____

4. _____

5. _____

Make a note of why each of these are important to you but it's OK if this surprises you because they will vary as you go through life. If, for example, your heart has been broken or you have had a great promotion, then love, trust and respect may go up the list and money might go to the bottom. Therefore, finding love, trust and respect again will be within your radar and money will take a back seat.

2. How do you use your values?

_____

_____

_____

_____

_____

_____

_____

_____

_____

We use our values as a guide to how we are living our life.

If you are struggling to find a solution to a problem or you don't know which decision to take, go back to your values and ask yourself:

3. How is this best serving me and the important things and people in my life?

_____

_____

_____

_____

And then ask the ever important,

4.   **Why?**

_____

_____

_____

_____

_____

_____

5.   **What are the benefits of this to the important things and people in my life?**

_____

_____

_____

_____

_____

_____

_____

6. Why?

_____

_____

_____

_____

_____

_____

_____

_____

_____

_____

The television presenter Davina McCall is a good example of how someone can turn their life around by going 'back to their values'. She talks openly about her family life, her uneven relationship with her mother and also about her heroin addiction in her twenties. For a while she was able to keep her heroin addiction under control, living a normal life by working a steady job so that nobody would suspect. The turning point came for her when she realised the heroin was really starting to spiral out of control and it started to affect how she lived her life. It was at this point that she went back to the values that her grandmother, her substitute mother, had instilled in her about living an honest, clean and decent life doing the best that she could do. It was this memory that helped her make the change in her life and seek help for her addiction.

Unfortunately, we often don't think about our values in this way until something goes drastically wrong, we are at a junction in our lives and we don't know which direction to go in. But they are worth keeping in mind at the main turning points, because being in tune with your values is an easy way of recognising where you stand today and where you could be standing tomorrow.[1,2,3,4,5]

" When the time comes you will know
You will feel it in your heart
And the only time you
will find real light
Is when you're searching in the dark. **"**

Someone, written by Lucy Spraggan

Strategy 2:
Hand on heart

Getting in touch with your feelings can be hard, especially when it is a subject that is close to your heart. I found connecting with heartfelt matters especially troublesome because I didn't like the feelings that it brought to me – buried, strong emotions were frightening and made me feel out of control. This 'hiding from the truth' is a habit that is hard to break. When we finally confront our feelings, we will come face to face with a lot of emotions that may make us uncomfortable. Hiding from these feelings is normal. Facing them and confronting them is the new normal – and at first it's terrifying!

Real and great change often only comes about when we are forced into it either by someone or something else, or we are in dire straits and the other alternative is extreme. For my dad, the change from male to female had to come about because the other alternative for him was to end his life. Thankfully, he didn't want to make his family suffer with losing him and he found the strength to confront the world with his secret and develop the life he had been longing for since he was five years old.

In 1987 gender dysphoria was not talked about. It was misunderstood and there was a lot of shame attached to it. For those reasons I was asked to keep the change a secret. The problem is that secrets weigh heavily on the mind, eventually increasing the production of stress hormones. The bigger the secret, the higher the risk[6].

At the age of forty, I felt eighty. My lower back ached so much I couldn't sleep properly; every time I rolled over in bed I would wake up with lower back pain and pain in my neck. I felt so stiff in the morning I used to have to roll out of bed. These aches and pains also contributed to my emotional state because I just couldn't understand what was happening. To me life wasn't beginning at forty; it felt like the end. In 2007 I stopped being able to function as a wife and mother effectively and I had to put my hand on my heart and acknowledge the root cause of my stress – my secret.

The counselling I received really helped. It helped me to start acknowledging some of the causes. Confronting my parents wasn't going to be straightforward; besides they were elderly, it wasn't fair, and there was no guarantee they would take on board my feelings or change their thought processes anyway. The only way I was going to start feeling better about life was to change my own feelings. It wasn't until I started my life coaching training that I really had to start asking myself the difficult questions I had been ignoring for so many years.

Honesty

'What was I REALLY thinking?'

If you can have a totally honest conversation with yourself, you can start to understand your thoughts and feelings and where they stem from. If you understand this then you are in a far better position to know where you want to get to, where you are now and what it is you need to do about it to start changing things to get from A to B.

Relationship breakdowns are most prevalent when families lack the ability to have honest conversations with each other. This may be due to the lack of trust and respect, or due to being frightened of the response they might get. Perhaps the family aren't in touch with their values and have lost the sight of what is important in their lives. Unfortunately it is common that not all families can have honest conversations. This can have consequences of varying degrees. Worst case? A son of a transsexual learnt about his father's male to female reassignment when he read it in the paper. The lack of honesty within this family resulted in the son committing suicide. A tragic life story which could have so easily been redirected with more trust and honesty within the family. So, my parents may have burdened me with a secret for many years, but they tried to be honest and I appreciate that.

During my research, as explained in Part 1, I discovered that my uncle John was relieved that his brother was only going to undergo transgender reassignment and nothing more serious was on the horizon. My mother's brother and sister-in-law wished they had been told sooner. The excuses that my mother had to make for my dad's late arrival at family events caused much concern and doubt in their minds. Once they knew the real story everything added up, their minds were put at rest and they could then support my mum with adjusting to her new normal. The lateness to family events was due to the time needed to change from Joan back to Martin. People are often far more understanding than you ever imagine.

Having a happy home life and a happy work life are important to keeping the balance and being able to love life and succeed. With the continual improvements to employment law it is important to speak to your boss as soon as possible so that they have a better understanding of what you are going through. An understanding boss, who is flexible, supportive and open minded is a huge bonus. You will never know until you approach them. Again, it is about having the honest conversations so that you know and they know where you both stand.

Open and honest conversations will encourage an 'open door policy' at work and at home. It will give you the space you need to be able to confront any potentially challenging issues head on, but also the mindset you need if confronted by others' less understanding, inflexible and closed minds. Whatever the situation, however OK you are with what is happening, there is always going to be someone who is going to push your buttons, stretch the truth and really dig the knife in. We all need our support network and the sooner we start to confront this the better.

YOUR SELF HELP SECTION

1. How am I really feeling?

_____

_____

_____

_____

_____

_____

2. What is it that I am really feeling?

_____

_____

_____

_____

_____

_____

_____

3. Why am I feeling this?

_____

_____

_____

_____

_____

_____

_____

4. What's the benefit of feeling this?

_____

_____

_____

_____

_____

_____

_____

5. **How is this affecting me?**

_____

_____

_____

_____

_____

_____

_____

6. **How is it affecting other people around me? (Family, friends, work colleagues)**

_____

_____

_____

_____

_____

_____

_____

7.   How is it affecting my relationships with these people?

_____

_____

_____

_____

_____

_____

_____

8.   What is the long-term effect of this?

_____

_____

_____

_____

_____

_____

_____

As I gradually incorporated my coaching into my teaching I made a vow to maintain total self-honesty. It wasn't until I was working with one client called Sharon on finding her truth, that she suddenly said: 'This is rather like having to put your hand on your heart?' and so I realised the power of this technique, and introduced it into my work. When I, or one of my clients, need to find the truth, we place our hand physically onto our heart – and it is easier to find your truth in that moment.

If this resonates with you, I challenge you to give it a try. Make plenty of time in a quiet place, place your hand on your heart – and go through these questions and write everything down. Put the work somewhere safe and share only when you are ready to. Or maybe never share it. That's fine: what is important is that you have started to download all the information you have been storing away. We can only emotionally store for so long without it affecting us in some way. Now you are letting it go.

9.   **When are you going to start downloading?**

_____

_____

_____

10. **If you were to download, how would this make you feel?**

_____

_____

_____

11. What are the benefits of feeling like this?

_____

_____

_____

_____

_____

_____

_____

"

Trust your beliefs
They are yours and yours alone
Trust your judgements and find your
own pace to thrive and succeed.

"

Cath Lloyd

Strategy 3:
Managing your belief system

Beliefs are what we uphold to be true about ourselves, about others, about science and religion. They help us make sense of the world and enable us to function.

There are three important steps in the development of our own belief systems.

Imprint period – up to our 7th year

When we are born we hold no belief system but we soon start learning about beliefs from our parents, other caregivers, our siblings. For example, when feeding an infant you will hear a parent say to their baby,

"You are such a good girl drinking all your milk."

Or as you grow up,

"You are such a mean child for not sharing. You must learn to share or else you will have no friends."

Small children are like sponges. They believe there is Santa Claus until they see their parents putting the presents under the tree or recognise their handwriting on the gift tags. When they reach the age of around twelve they develop or feed these beliefs in different ways. They absorb what people say, what they read or see, and the emotions and insecurities they feel associated with those. Therefore, emotions equal knowledge. But how true are they?

Modelling period – 8th to 13th year

As children grow they start to copy highly influential people such as parents, teachers and maybe sports or dance instructors. I remember when my children were growing up and they started to answer the phone. When my son answered the phone he was almost like an exact copy of his dad. The words he used and the way he paced around the house whilst he talked. In contrast, my daughter mimicked me even to the extent of the phrasing of her sentences.

Socialisation period – 13th to 21st year

Young people are influenced by their peers and people they admire and start to relate to and bond with people who share their likes and interests. It is at this stage in life that young people are also starting to develop their own values and belief systems. They may turn away from the earlier programming that they were in contact with. Their beliefs are also affected by how others respond to them.

What can a limiting belief system do?

A child who is struggling academically might feel his parents or teachers' disapproval when they say things such as:

- You haven't done very well again have you?
- You're not like your brothers and sisters, are you?
- We are disappointed in you.
- You never try hard enough.

This is a very similar scenario for people in abusive relationships, which can be seen in the workplace as well as in private lives.

All this negativity will build up over the years and will be forced into the subconscious mind. These will be triggered when the subconscious hears other similar words, phrases, tones of voice or even smells associated with the past.

The thing is, our memories don't know what is true or false. Subconsciously we will only remember what we want to remember and then squeeze that into a memory that suits our belief system. Unfortunately, we can easily forget all the good things that have happened, such as other things you are good at, so our kindness and caring nature will slip away without being recognised by us. Our memories are very fickle and we have to rebuild our belief systems by challenging them, by putting our hands on our hearts and being totally honest with ourselves.

It is a hard process but a vital one, for our beliefs affect our thought processes which then affect our actions and how we manage difficult situations.

When does a belief become a limiting belief?

It becomes a limiting belief when we:

- Lose confidence in our abilities and don't push ourselves towards what we really want
- Don't get out of a destructive relationship
- Make excuses for why something didn't happen, like we didn't get a positive response we were hoping for
- Think there is no point in setting ourselves a goal because we assume we won't achieve it
- Go into destructive thoughts and can't see the positive in anything that we do

But how do we know they are true?

We believe them to be true because we have collected, processed, saved and regurgitated how others have responded to us. We will stay locked in the same cycle unless we analyse and change our thought processes.

YOUR SELF HELP SECTION

1. What do you believe to be true about yourself?

_____

_____

_____

_____

_____

_____

2. Where did this belief come from?

_____

_____

_____

_____

_____

_____

_____

3. **How do you know it to be true?**

_____

_____

_____

_____

_____

_____

_____

4. **What proof is there?**

_____

_____

_____

_____

_____

_____

_____

Just because we have formed a habit around these beliefs it doesn't mean that you can't change them.

5. **Pick one of the limiting beliefs you hold about yourself.**

_____

_____

_____

_____

6. **Write down everything you know about that belief, who said it, the evidence, your feelings around it and how it makes you behave.**

_____

_____

_____

_____

_____

_____

_____

_____

_____

7. What would you like to think, feel and behave like instead?

_____

_____

_____

_____

_____

_____

_____

8. How would you like it to be different?

_____

_____

_____

_____

_____

_____

_____

9. Think back over your life and find examples of better, happier beliefs and write them down.

_____

_____

_____

_____

_____

_____

10. What else is there to reinforce this new, better and happier belief?

_____

_____

_____

_____

_____

_____

Other ideas to support your new belief system

- Make up a vision board around how you want to be different. See it in colour and see the words that represent this.

- Be more aware of your new belief and how you can reinforce it and feed that belief like you were nurturing a baby so that each day it becomes stronger. This isn't about showing off; it is about quietly knowing that you are better than that limiting belief in your old thinking pattern.

- That old limiting belief will rear its ugly head from time to time, especially at times when something takes you by surprise. Be assertive with it: tell it it's not being helpful to you and tell it go so far away that it is a tiny speck of dust way out in the distance.

- Keep feeding yourself with gratitude, being around positive people who see the good in you.

" **Maybe the reason that some people have a hard time believing I'm happy is that, until recently, I've had a hard time believing it myself.** "

Professor Green, English rapper, singer, songwriter and author of *Lucky*[7]

Strategy 4:
Stop playing the victim

It took me a long time to admit, but I spent a lot of years playing the victim. My reaction to my dad's gender reassignment became the thing that every relationship revolved around, be it at home or work. I was so frightened about how people might react, what they might think and say that I spent my whole time keeping a check on the solidity of the barrier I had built around me. A lot of the time we are unaware of playing the victim, until it is pointed out to us or we start realising we want something different from life. People often play the victim because they are getting something useful from it, perhaps something like:

- An air of importance
- Getting attention
- Being different
- A reason to be angry or sad, or eat and drink unhealthily
- A reason not to accept and not to move on

When you look at these written down it seems obvious, but when we are stuck in the narrow frame of mind where we can't see past our own issues, it can be difficult to see the light.

There are many examples of playing the victim. A good one is when you listen to the people around you like friends or work colleagues and think:

- I have applied for thousands of jobs and I never get them.
- I always end up in a dead-end relationship.

- The examiner must hate me because I never do very well in exams.
- Good things always happen to other people, never to me.
- Something is going to go wrong because life is too good at the moment.

Have a think about your life and the difficult issues that you have dealt with in the past or are dealing with at present. How do you feel about them?

Are you a CAUSE or an EFFECT person?

If you are a CAUSE person that means, "I caused this, this is the result of my actions and I can change this."

If you are an EFFECT person, "It is their fault and I am the victim here."

I felt like the victim because I didn't choose for my dad to have transgender reassignment. His actions made me feel like this and it is his actions that have made me struggle for all these years.

As you can see I CAUSED those feelings because I didn't know how to handle them at the time and I chose to hold onto them and to let them go unchallenged. I was so caught up in these feelings I couldn't see how to make it different, to find someone who could help me. Deep down I knew that if I did challenge them I would have to deal with the aftermath of all those feelings and emotions that I didn't like within myself. I was living as an EFFECT person.

In actual fact, playing the victim takes up a lot of negative thought processing, energy and time. It makes you feel resentful and negative, towards a lot of people who probably don't deserve it, it saps your energy when you could be doing something positive, useful and fun, and it also ages you.

YOUR SELF HELP SECTION

1. When you go about your day spot the resentful and negative people who you encounter.

2. What is their posture like?

_____

_____

_____

_____

3. Look at their complexion, the way they speak and the way they go about their day.

4. What do you notice about them?

_____

_____

_____

_____

_____

_____

5. **Do you want to be like them?**

_____

6. **Why?**

_____

_____

_____

_____

_____

_____

_____

_____

When feeling resentful or hurt over something, perhaps from some-one's actions or words, there is a great set of questions to take yourself through to start discovering a way out of the trap of being the victim.

7. **Am I playing the victim?**

_____

8. Why do I play that role?

_____

_____

_____

_____

_____

9. Why has it upset me so much?

_____

_____

_____

_____

10. What does it give me that I might not get if I didn't play the victim?

_____

_____

_____

_____

_____

11. **What are the long-term benefits from playing this role?**

_____

_____

_____

_____

12. **What if I weren't playing the victim any longer, what would I be feeling?**

_____

_____

_____

_____

13. **What if I weren't playing the victim any longer, how would I be behaving?**

_____

_____

_____

_____

_____

14. **How would life be better for me?**

_____

_____

_____

_____

_____

_____

> " It's funny, all the things that
> used to niggle at me have become
> a lot less irritating now I don't
> pay them any attentions. "

Professor Green, in *Lucky*[8]

Strategy 5:
Laws of attraction

The way our minds work is amazing. The mind is such a powerful organ; will scientists ever fully understand the extent at which the brain processes the amount of information it does? How it changes it and reinforces the variety of ideas, images and creativity that we have? What we experience isn't necessarily what we remember. We can trick our brain into thinking something that hasn't happened took place, just by pretending we truly believe it. How is it that we can take a tablet knowing it is a placebo but still our bodies react to it? How is it that some people can go through a life-threatening accident and come out of it almost unscathed? Others can struggle and suffer for the rest of their lives with something far less serious. How is it that someone can lift the weight of a car singlehanded to rescue a child?

It is all to do with the power of the mind and it has no limitations that we know of.

When we talk about the 'laws of attraction', what we are referring to is how our mind reacts to what we are thinking, seeing and hearing. Our thought reprocesses have a huge impact on how and what we achieve in life. If, for example, I believed (as I did) that I was a disappointment at school, I then fed that belief by saying to myself:

"Well, I'm not surprised my parents were disappointed in me because I always did rubbish at my spelling tests when I was eight. That's why I got smacked on the legs and the other teachers always made a comment about my abilities compared to my sister. So, if I'm rubbish at school then I will be rubbish at everything I do. That's

why I was two points off getting a distinction in my Art Foundation Course and that's why I didn't get a first in my degree. I don't try hard enough and I'm just not good enough."

How long do you keep this thinking up? For the rest of your life?

Some, who really can't see the better part of themselves, may decide that taking their own life is the only option. A tragic end to a life.

Even when others tell you that you're not rubbish, it's easier to swish those kind words of support away with a, *"They're just saying that, they don't really mean it"*, or, *"don't be daft it's just luck"*, or even worse, *"it's not down to me, it's the other members of the team; they need to take the credit."* At the end of the day there is no such thing as luck. We make our own luck and make our own destiny.

The way we think is what we attract. If we wake up in the morning and imagine it is going to be a bad day and everything is going to go wrong, then the betting is that is what will happen. Even if something wonderful happens it won't be remembered because the mind is so fixated on only seeing things that go wrong. So, what would happen if you turned this the other way and you wake up in the morning saying that it is going to be a great day. Well you would notice all the great things and be able to reason out the things that didn't go so well during the day. Doesn't that sound great? I'm not saying that if you only thought in a positive way you would never get any bad days, because that would just be unrealistic. It is how you manage your thought processes and think things through rather going straight into melt-down because you stubbed your toe on the leg of the bed as soon as you got up in the morning.

To change your law of attraction is about reflecting on your thought processes, listening to the chat inside your head and deciding how you want it to be different. If you decide you are a negative thought processor, then change it. However, you do have to recognise your thinking which can be difficult at first. But when you do recognise the negative thought process it is telling your mind to, "Stop. Shut up. You're not being helpful to me." Then you can repro-cess that information in a positive way.

Thinking in a more positive way

"I always end up in bad relationships; they never last long and they are always disruptive. It is so unfair; why does everyone else have a great long lasting relationship?"

Could be changed to:

"There seems to be a pattern here with my love relationships. I would like to be in a happier relationship with someone who is going to love me for who I am. What do I need to look for in a partner that I haven't been getting?"

Recognising that there is a problem in the first place is a great starting point but then it's how you process it. Thinking about how you want a relationship to be is a great place to start, and then you are in a better position to start looking for what you want. This will mean you are less likely to be the victim and start taking control over the situations.

YOUR SELF HELP SECTION

1. As you go about your day keep a check on your thought processes and write down anything that stands out.

2. At the end of the day what do you notice about them?

   _____

   _____

   _____

   _____

   _____

   _____

3. How did they make you feel?

   _____

   _____

   _____

   _____

   _____

   _____

4. **How would you like to feel instead?**

_____

_____

_____

_____

_____

5. **How could they be more positive?**

_____

_____

_____

_____

_____

6. **What words could you use instead?**

_____

_____

_____

_____

Make up a gratitude diary for yourself. You can do this on paper, on the computer or your phone. At the end of each day, reflect on what has happened during the day and write down at least three good things. The obvious ones are that you are grateful for the love of your family, the food on your table, that you are fit and healthy. Yes, these are important and will probably go down at the beginning when you start diarising these thoughts. The next step is to go beyond that because you will always be grateful for those things. Start looking at the smaller things that are happening around you, for example:

- I had a great conversation with a stranger on my commute into work today.
- A colleague at work could see I was upset because I was finding a piece of work difficult and they asked if they could help me.
- It was lovely to go out for a walk and feel the sunshine on my face today.
- When I woke up this morning I could hear the birds singing.

Often in life it is the little things that enrich our lives, making the hard days easier and helping us put into perspective the whole picture of our existence.

Some days will be harder than others, especially at the beginning, or if you are going through a particularly trying time, but keep going because it will be worth it. This exercise, if you persist, will be a great tool when you are struggling because it will help you see a brighter light to get through those dark days. It will help you to feel less of a victim so that you can be in greater control of your feelings.

"Look for what you want in your life and you will see it. When you see it, live it."

" You gotta pack up your
troubles in your old kit bag
And bury them beneath the sea
I don't care what the people may say
What the people may say about me. "

Pack Up, written by Timothy Daniel Woodcock, Felix Powell, Eliza
Sophie Caird, George Asaf, George H Powell and Matthew Prime

Strategy 6:
Acceptance

We all know the great saying, *"Life is a like a roller coaster, full of ups, downs, twists and turns."* You either embrace it or you fight against it. The majority of us like our lives to run smoothly but things will happen that will test us, challenge us, frustrate us, make us cry – but also life will also throw at us great times of joy, happiness, excitement, adventure and curiosity. We can't have one without the other.

When we are so caught up in difficult and troubling times it can be difficult to be able to accept what is going on around us. The thing is, like playing the victim, our body is using up an excessive amount of energy just trying to keep us going with some sort of normality. The lack of acceptance will generate a whole host of challenging conversations or arguments in our head and will eventually pay a price on our mental and physical health. These mind games that we are creating within ourselves will also be stopping us from concentrating on greater things, which could give us joy, rewards and long-term happiness.

It took me twenty-five years to really start accepting the change that my dad had gone through. I spent those years kidding myself that it was all going to be ok but deep down it was still niggling away in my subconscious, until my mental and physical health was challenged. It was only then that I started to consciously challenge my mindset.

Acceptance as a powerful tool

Watching someone you love such as a parent, partner, friend or child fade away is an extremely painful process. How does a child accept their parents separating when everything appeared to be happy to them? Even more difficult must be having to accept a sudden death through a tragic accident, murder or suicide. It will leave those affected with a mixture of feelings:

1. Guilt for being alive, fit, well and healthy
2. Guilt for wanting them to die so that they are free from pain and suffering
3. Loss is difficult to accept and painful so wanting them to survive to make life better for yourself
4. Anger – why should it be them? They have been a good person all their life and why not someone who has murdered, raped and abused others
5. Anger because the one you love is being taken from you

How do you accept something that you don't know the reason for? How do we accept something that we never asked for?

We all think, feel and behave uniquely; therefore, the solution is an individual process. However, one thing is for sure – if we don't start to accept the facts as they are, we are going to be living a life of misery. That misery will not only affect us as individuals but the people who are around us. Feelings are transmitted subconsciously because they affect everything that we do. How we express ourselves, verbally and physically. How we connect and build relationships with others and the energy we put into our everyday lives.

It's rather like agreeing to disagree. We know we feel a particular way but then we have to acknowledge it, accept it and then decide how we want to feel instead. The important part of any of this is to learn from it. If we don't learn, we will never discover the answers to the big why question.

YOUR SELF HELP SECTION

Before you start, use the hand on your heart technique to find the honest answers to these questions. Don't just think about them, write them down and put them away somewhere safe, away from prying eyes. These are your thoughts and your thoughts alone until you are ready to share them.

1. **Why did this happen?**

_____

_____

_____

_____

2. **How did it make me feel?**

_____

_____

_____

_____

_____

_____

3. **What effect has this had on me?**

_____

_____

_____

_____

_____

4. **What effect has this had on other people around me?**

_____

_____

_____

_____

5. **What could have been different?**

_____

_____

_____

_____

_____

6. How did I handle it?

_____

_____

_____

_____

7. Who could I turn to for support if something like this happens again?

_____

_____

_____

_____

8. How will I recognise these feelings and behaviours again?

_____

_____

_____

_____

9. **What can I do to reduce the risk of this happening again?**

_____

_____

_____

_____

_____

_____

_____

10. **What have I learned from this experience?**

_____

_____

_____

_____

_____

_____

_____

11. **What are the benefits of having experienced this in my life?**

_____

_____

_____

_____

_____

_____

_____

12. **What are the benefits if I do not accept this?**

_____

_____

_____

_____

_____

_____

_____

There are going to be times when you will revert back to the habit of those old feelings – perhaps when you are under stress, tired or low. Relapse is normal; it happens to us all and it is again about accepting this relapse. Don't chastise yourself for it; go back to the questions and answer them again with an open and honest heart so that you can start to get back to moving forwards.

Acceptance of a situation doesn't mean you will forget. Understanding it better will enable you to live a happier life with less burdens to carry wherever you go. One of the techniques I teach people, once they have begun to move on, is how to just 'let it go'. Let those feelings and emotions go free instead of keeping them bound up inside of you. Let them go into the atmosphere so they will disperse naturally and leave you free to think and feel happier versions.

" **Go out and flutter your wings and glide into life.** "

Man into Woman: The First Sex Change, edited by Niels Hoyer[9]

Strategy 7:
Strategise your strategy for change

By now you will have revealed some truths about your own mindset and thought processes. The big step now is to get adventurous and get active. It is really tempting to learn all this, nod your head wisely and plan to take action. Then life gets in the way and we realise how busy and tiring it is just doing all the usual: go to work, walk the dog, take the kids to football or ballet and then there's the cooking and the household chores. Before we realise what has happened we have forgotten what we learned and we are back to page one and square one. How do we avoid this setback? We break down our goal into baby steps, which will take us to where we want to go in tiny, manageable ways whilst we live our lives and find our footing.

In 2007 when my feelings were bouncing around uncontrollably, I started to do my life coaching training. It put me in a great position to start taking control but that was only the start of my new journey. It still took me a long while to organise and come up with my own personal strategies that support my thought processes. I still need to use them sometimes but I know that when I need them they are there waiting so I can pick them up and change my outlook. You will hear a lot of people talking about how important positive thinking is and that you should be positive all of the time. Well, this is an unrealistic view to take in life. Even the most positive of people are going to have bad days when they just want to curl up in a ball and hide away from the world. Instead of positive thinking I would like to share with you a term I have adopted from a wonderful new author, Deb Hawken, and her book *Who Am I, Where Am I, What Is This Place?*, which is constructive thinking. I love this phrase because it is about building a new foundation to give us the strength to adjust the foundations of our thought processes and build on top a great construction of support for ourselves.

How does this approach help us build? Take losing your job. Over the last twenty years almost all of us will have experienced job loss or redundancy. Losing your job is heart wrenching, leaving people angry, bewildered and at a loss for what to do next. These are all natural feelings and can leave people in a place of self-pity. This self-pity is fine for a short while, but over a long period of time can manifest into stress and even depression. However, to be able to make a healthy move forwards to the next phase there is a process for each of us. The sooner we start to get that process moving the sooner we will be in a better position. To manage these uncomfortable feelings, we must try to ignore them and start organising ourselves. The first important part is to accept all the help and support that is offered to us. At the time, you might feel that it is useless but you never know what you might discover unless you accept the help and take from it what you can.

Retirement is a huge key change in people's lives when they have been working for forty plus years. Retirement should be a time to relish your leisure time but it is a known fact that some professions more than others have a short retirement life. After working within a career that has given them a clear regime some can feel lost, out of place and living a life of no purpose any longer.

Big change needs to bring with it large and open minded thinking processes to help find the next phase of life that will be as fulfilling as the previous years.

So let's get started on constructing the strategy you need to make the changes that you want to see in yourself.

YOUR SELF HELP SECTION

Map your mind

I love mind maps because you can get into a real creative flow. In the first instance it is better if you can do this live rather than on the computer. The main aim of this exercise is to get the information down on paper so that you can see it in all its glory, exploring and itemising the things you are good at and the areas in need of improvement or adjustment.

Equipment

Get a large sheet of paper, coloured pens and if you want post it notes so that you can move your ideas and thoughts around if you want to.

1. In the centre of the page put your main focus in one or two words or you could use a picture instead that represents where you want to be going in life. Make it vibrant and colourful so that it really stands out and you enjoy looking at it.

2. This is where you go back to connecting with your self-honesty levels. Put you hand on your heart, shut your eyes if you want to and take a few moments just to listen and feel your breathing and think about what needs to happen to make this better for yourself and the people around you. How can you change this? What do you need to do to make it different? To make it the way you really want it?

3. Start building around this centre point with coloured arms for different areas you want to develop. These might be things like: wellness, happiness, positive attitude, confidence levels, honesty, commitment, relationships, career, skills, qualifications, holidays, hobbies or your children. It can be anything you want it to be because this is about you, for you. However, now this is important, you must have a SUPPORT heading.

4. Now start branching out from there for each section. Just write things down; you may be jumping about from one sub-heading to another but that is ok. If you wait till later you might have forgotten that important thought. You might find you need to link some of those sub-headings together with arrows.

5. Write everything down that has gone through your thoughts. When these thoughts have dried up, shut your eyes again, put your hand on your heart, concentrate on your breathing and think, what else? Write it all down, even the things that you think are insignificant and not worth mentioning.

6. Take a look at what you have written. What do you notice about it? What one thing from that list could you commit to immediately? Highlight it.

Nothing will change if you don't start taking action and being methodical about it. Doing it one day and not the next three days will make for slow progress. That's why doing a little bit every day will give you effective changes which are a great way forwards. Put that commitment into action.

Once I started to work on making big positive changes to the way I felt about myself and how I wanted to behave, a work colleague of mine suddenly passed comment on my "new positive outlook on life".

You know what my thought was? With a smile on my face.

Yes, I'm loving it and I'm going to keep it this way.

YOUR SELF HELP SECTION

Each day record it. This is where you need to give yourself time each day. Making a big change in the way you feel and behave is rather like giving yourself a new project to work on. Recording it will not only help you sift through your feelings and behaviours but also help you to download controversial thoughts and feelings that will be flitting in and out of your consciousness. Don't get hung up on your spelling, grammar or punctuation: this isn't an exam, nobody is going to come along and mark it, just get it out of your head and down on paper. If you keep them stored up in your head, it is taking up valuable thought processes that will reinforce the wrong neuron connections. What you are trying to do here is understand what your processes are so that you can learn from them and change them. Reflect and learn from the not so good. Relish in the good, enabling you to gather more of that to help you build the right neuron connections in the brain and stomach. So, these are the questions you need to ask yourself:

1. **What went well today?**

   _____

   _____

2. **Why?**

   _____

   _____

   _____

   _____

3. What didn't go so well today?

_____

_____

4. Why?

_____

_____

_____

5. How could I do things differently to make it easier on myself, be more effective, be more positive?

_____

_____

_____

6. What have I done successfully in the past that could support me in this?

_____

_____

_____

7.   **Who could I seek support from?**

_____

_____

_____

8.   **What support do I need to help me?**

_____

_____

_____

Learn from each new day, so before you go to bed each night or first thing in the morning, write down your main, positive objective for the next day.

As you go through this process you will start to notice a difference in how you are feeling and behaving. At the end of each week read over what you have written to see your journey so far. At first you might find the writing tiresome and lengthy but give way to it. Allow your thoughts to flow as if you had the perfect listener in front of you. Someone who will not interrupt you when you are in full flow or judge you when you are feeling vulnerable.

When you are starting to feel comfortable with the first adjustment to your life, pick your next objective and so on. Once you start it is amazing how quickly your emotions, feelings and behaviours will change and others will be able to see it and start to comment on it.

“ People are like stained glass windows. They sparkle and shine when the sun is out but when the darkness sets in their true beauty is revealed only if there is a light from within. ”

Dr. Elisabeth Kübler-Ross, Swiss-American psychiatrist, pioneer in near-death studies, author of *On Death and Dying*[10]

Conclusion

Dad changing to Joan thirty years ago was an ordeal for the whole family and we have each dealt with it with varying degrees of success. However, when my sister announced her divorce in 2009, it brought home to my parents and those surrounding them just how strong their own relationships were. Despite everything, Annie and Joan had proved they could weather any storm and retained a tremendous amount of love for each other. And the rest of us couldn't help but see and feel it too.

These days Mum and Joan are companions and to see them walk down the street together they would look like any two friends. However, Mum will refer to Joan as her 'partner' should the need arise. Joan calls me her daughter and when people now refer to my two mums I just let it ride. It's taken a long time to be able to do that and at first I had to come to terms with what I'd lost. On the odd occasion someone will ask about our relationship and who they are to each other. I now say, "Anne is my mum and Joan is my dad; he had trans-gender reassignment."

Through Dad's transition I've lost the person who would be seen as the head of the household and I've lost the right to say 'my mum and my dad'. That's something we all take for granted and it only matters when it's gone. It has taken a lot to redefine the relationships between us all but finally we've all become closer than ever. I now see my parents five days a week and I've got a renewed respect for them both as individuals. Most importantly I now have genuine respect for Joan rather than this person who used to be my dad. Her journey has taken an enormous amount of courage.

I now have a very different sort of closeness with my mum. She suffers from Alzheimer's and I want to make the most of the time I have with her and enjoy helping her manage her memory loss and supporting her on a day to day basis. As we wait for doctors' appointments together, we share a memory from the past, and we laugh about it. A favourite of ours is: one warm sunny July day in the mid 1970s my sister and I had been up the garden secretly picking the peas, storing them in our toy suitcases.

"Girls, what have you got in your suitcases?" Mum asked.

In unison we both held up our suitcase with a little shake and answered, "Felt pens Mummy!" That was close! We chuckled together, happy we had got away with that one. Little did we know that our parents had spotted the empty pea pods in the compost.

Regarding gender reassignment, thankfully there is so much more openness today, whether that is through the media, films, social media or novels tackling a wide range of related issues. The attitude of the general public has changed considerably over the last thirty years. Look at the reaction of my children when I finally gathered the courage to tell them about their granddad. To them it was normal. They had known nothing else and this is the same for millions of others. In general, as a nation we are a lot more open, honest and are having more constructive conversations about difficult subjects than we ever had before.

Since her operations Joan has undertaken a lot of great work supporting other transsexuals through the process of change. Supporting and listening to them, helping them understand their feelings, how the process of change will progress, how to communicate with their families and work colleagues and sometimes visiting them in hospital. She has worked tirelessly supporting the registered charity 'GIRES' (Gender Identity Research and Education Society). The change of passports was already recognised but the work she undertook for the Gender Recognition Act 2004 has made huge differences to so many individuals to be able to live a more normal life as their natural gender. This has been a huge step forwards with the issuing of the new birth certificate, employment law that now officially recognises the individual's new gender, and marriage between same sex couples.

As for me, I had been thrust into something I had only seen talked about on the TV probably in the early 1980s. However, this has made the person I am today. My quest in life is to now help the unheard be heard, the voiceless find their voice, so that they can make the change from stress to success. If you follow my '7 steps to living your new normal' you will find your way. The right way for you.

YOUR SELF HELP SECTION – REFLECT

Before we finish I would just like to recap on the strategies and remind you of where you need to start in order to make huge differences to living your normal.

Strategy 1:

The importance of our values

1. What are your values?
2. How do you use those values?
3. How is this best serving you and the important things and people in your life?
4. Why?
5. What are the benefits of this to the important things and people in my life?
6. Why?

Strategy 2:

Hand on heart

1. How am I really feeling?
2. What is it that I am really feeling?
3. Why am I feeling this?
4. What's the benefit of feeling this?
5. How is this affecting me?
6. How is it affecting other people around me? (Family, friends, work colleagues)

7. How is it affecting my relationships with these people?
8. What is the long-term effect of this?
9. When are you going to start downloading?
10. If you were to download, how would this make you feel?
11. What are the benefits of feeling like this?

Strategy 3:

Managing your belief system

1. What do you believe to be true about yourself?
2. Where did this belief come from?
3. How do you know it to be true?
4. What proof is there?
5. Pick one of the limiting beliefs you hold about yourself.
6. Write down everything you know about that belief, who said it, the evidence, your feelings around it and how it makes you behave.
7. What would you like to think, feel and behave like instead?
8. How would you like it to be different?
9. Think back over your life and find examples of better, happier beliefs and write them down.
10. What else is there to reinforce this new, better and happier belief?

Other ideas to support your new belief system

- Make up a vision board around how you want to be different. See it in colour and see the words that represent this.

- Be more aware of your new belief and how you can reinforce it and feed that belief like you were nurturing a baby so that each day it becomes stronger. This isn't about showing off; it is about quietly knowing that you are better than that limiting belief in your old thinking pattern.

- That old limiting belief will rear its ugly head from time to time, especially at times when something takes you by surprise. Be assertive with it: tell it it's not being helpful to you and tell it go so far away that it is a tiny speck of dust way out in the distance.

- Keep feeding yourself with gratitude, being around positive people who see the good in you.

Strategy 4:

Stop playing the victim

1. When you go about your day spot the resentful and negative people who you encounter.
2. What is their posture like?
3. Look at their complexion, the way they speak and the way they go about their day.
4. What do you notice about them?
5. Do you want to be like them?
6. Why?
7. Am I playing the victim?
8. Why do I play that role?
9. Why has it upset me so much?
10. What does it give me that I might not get if I didn't play the victim?
11. What are the long-term benefits from playing this role?
12. What if I weren't playing the victim any longer, what would I be feeling?
13. What if I weren't playing the victim any longer, how would I be behaving?
14. How would life be better for me?

Strategy 5:

Laws of attraction

1. As you go about your day keep a check on your thought processes and write down anything that stands out.
2. At the end of the day what do you notice about them?
3. How did they make you feel?
4. How would you like to feel instead?
5. How could they be more positive?
6. What words could you use instead?

Strategy 6:

Acceptance

1. Why did this happen?
2. How did it make me feel?
3. What effect has this had on me?
4. What effect has this had on other people around me?
5. What could have been different?
6. How did I handle it?
7. Who could I turn to for support if something like this happens again?
8. How will I recognise these feelings and behaviours again?
9. What can I do to reduce the risk of this happening again?
10. What have I learned from this experience?
11. What are the benefits of having experienced this in my life?
12. What are the benefits if I do not accept this?

Strategy 7:

Strategise your strategy for change

1. Set up your mind map with a focal point in the centre of the page.
2. Add your subheadings.
3. Add all your ideas and thoughts around how to progress in each area.
4. Start with one item off this map to concentrate on.
5. Reflect and record the outcomes of the progression of each change daily and ask yourself the following questions:

   - What went well today?
   - Why?
   - What didn't go so well today?
   - Why?
   - How could I do things differently to make it easier on myself, be more effective, be more positive?
   - What have I done successfully in the past that could support me in this?
   - Who could I seek support from?
   - What support do I need to help me?

6. Learn from each new day, so before you go to bed each night or first thing in the morning, write down your main, positive objective for the next day.

Endnotes

1. Davina McCall interview with Michael Parkinson 2008 BBC
2. www.youtube.com/watch?v=PSWOIuDPVSk
3. Davina McCall interview on *This Morning* 2016 ITV
4. Davina McCall interview on *This Morning* 2016 ITV
5. https://www.youtube.com/watch?v=9YzJAOXRqQo
6. https://www.forbes.com/sites/nextavenue/2013/10/24/keeping-secrets-can-be-hazardous-to-your-health/#2ed1f1e360bd *'Keeping Secrets Can Be Hazardous To Your Health'*, by Gina Roberts-Grey, 24th October 2013
7. Page 233; published by Blink Publishing
8. Page 233; published by Blink Publishing
9. Spoken by Werner Kretz as quoted in the book *Man Into Woman: The First Sex Change, A portrait of Lili Elbe*, edited by Niels Hoyer
10. Quote taken from http://www.ekrfoundation.org/

Biography

I come from a teaching background in adult education; it was meant to be a temporary arrangement but ended up spanning over twenty-five years. I realised very quickly that I enjoyed helping others to achieve their best and concentrated my efforts there. I enjoyed the creative side of making pottery but teaching was satisfying on a deeper level. The last fifteen years I taught in offender learning. This experience thrust me into a very different society that helped me refine my teaching and life coaching skills whilst keeping me very much in touch with the real and creative worlds. Through sharing of skills and engaging in conversation to support my students to make better pots, paint better pictures, be better parents and be more successful individuals through looking at their life from a different angle.

As a life coach, I can support individuals and groups of people so much more effectively. I can combine my teaching and life coaching skills with a holistic approach, where the education system restricted me.

We all have a story to tell and mine is through my journey of acceptance when my dad became Joan. The combination of my life's journey and my teaching experiences has helped me to notice individuality a lot more clearly. It has helped me to see that, for some, life is often not as easy as they would like it to be. It can be complicated but at other times we make it more complicated than it needs to be. All these complications can throw us off balance, make us feel weird and want to shout from the tree tops, "All I want is to feel normal!"

If this resonates with you then I can support you in finding your feelings of normal again. As a client of mine I will help you to acknowledge and under-stand your feelings more easily. I will support you in finding your normal so that you can start preparing your actions. I will take you on a journey where you will be able to learn more about effective breathing, mindfulness, gratitude, acceptance, acknowledgement and listening to your inner self through self-honesty.

I work with individuals and groups but also put on retreats and Stress Relief Awareness Days.

To find out more go to:
www.cathlloyd.co.uk

For day to day connection, join me on Facebook at
https://www.facebook.com/CLmakethechange

and

www.facebook.com/ – living with normal
Instagram – lloydcath
LinkedIn – Catherine Lloyd

Join me on your journey to living your normal.

Your Life is Your Choice. Choose The Best Way Not The Easiest Way.

Cath Lloyd

" One day you will wake up and realise that life has passed you by, that your dreams of today are gone, that the things you wanted are no longer there.

Not today.
Not now.
Not your life.

This is the day where you take control and create your future. Life isn't about waiting, hoping or wishing. It is about creating, doing and truly living.
Today is that day. "

Brad Gast, Dean of Business & Industry and Continuing Education at Northcentral Technical College, USA.

Lightning Source UK Ltd.
Milton Keynes UK
UKOW07f0611281117
313486UK00003B/13/P

9 780995 739086